The Economics of Market Dominance

The Economics of
Market Dominance

Edited by
DONALD HAY AND **JOHN VICKERS**

Basil Blackwell

© D. A. Hay and J. S. Vickers 1987

First published 1987

Basil Blackwell Ltd
108 Cowley Road, Oxford, OX4 1JF, UK

Basil Blackwell Inc.
432 Park Avenue South, Suite 1503
New York, NY 10016, USA

British Library Cataloguing in Publication Data

The Economics of market dominance.
1. International business enterprises
I. Hay, Donald A.   II. Vickers, John
338.8′8   HD2755.5
ISBN 0-631-14784-5

Library of Congress Cataloging in Publication Data
The Economics of market dominance.
"This volume is the outcome of a conference on the economics of market dominance held at Nuffield College, Oxford, in September 1985"—Pref.
Bibliography: p.
Includes index.
1. Industrial organization (Economic theory)—
Congresses. 2. Monopolies—Congresses. I. Hay, Donald A. II. Vickers, John, 1958–
HD2326.E24 1987   338.8′2   86-26416
ISBN 0-631-14784-5

Typeset in Times on 10/12 pt
by DMB (Typesetting) Oxford
Printed in Great Britain
by Billing and Sons Ltd, Worcester.

Contents

Preface

This volume is the outcome of a conference on the economics of market dominance held at Nuffield College, Oxford in September 1985. We are grateful to the college for providing a congenial environment for our discussions.

The expenses of the conference were covered by a grant from the National Economic Research Associates. We wish to record our appreciation of their generous assistance, without which it would have been extremely difficult to call the conference.

Versions of the five contributed papers in the volume were presented at the conference. We are particularly grateful to those speakers who came from overseas, making time in very busy personal schedules to do so. We extend our thanks too to the 25 participants – academics and practitioners from government and the legal world – who provided a lively discussion of issues arising from the papers. The authors then responded to requests for revisions with good grace and alacrity.

The first paper in the volume was written by us, after the conference, in order to set the scene for the contributed papers, and to present our own reflections on the major issues raised at the conference and in the papers. We are grateful to Tom Sharpe for detailed comments on an earlier draft. Neither he, nor any of the conference participants, bears any responsibility for the contents.

Donald Hay,
Jesus College, Oxford
John Vickers,
Nuffield College, Oxford

1

The Economics of Market Dominance

JOHN VICKERS AND DONALD HAY

The Problem of Market Dominance

The theme of this book is market dominance – the power of a single firm or group of firms over the supply of goods or services in a market or set of markets. As a phenomenon it is neither new nor surprising. Monopolistic market structures and their consequences have for long been part of established economic analysis, and governments have designed monopoly policies to deal with them in practice. However, real-world monopolies do not always fit the textbook categories, and their persistence in the face of monopoly policies raises questions about those policies. The matter has been brought to a head in recent years by cases initiated by antitrust authorities against allegedly monopolistic firms in technologically progressive industries. These cases have served to highlight the inadequacies of traditional monopoly analysis; they have also engaged the talents of many specialists in industrial economics. From these cases has emerged a much better understanding of dominant firms. The objective of this book is to explain the new analysis to a wider audience, and in particular to suggest implications for the principles and practice of policy towards dominant firms.

   This introductory chapter is intended to provide a guide to these new developments, as a framework for understanding the original papers which make up the rest of this book. The second section of this chapter sketches the new analysis, in both its positive and its normative aspects, under the headings of the exercise, the acquisition, and the maintenance of dominance. The third section suggests a set of principles which should be applied in constructing an effective policy. These are then deployed in the fourth section, which contains a brief description and evaluation of competition policy in the UK, the EEC, and the US. The comparison serves to indicate the important differences in policy in the three jurisdictions. It also suggests that the UK and Europe have a lot to learn from the US. That section also explores two aspects of policy that give rise for concern in all three jurisdictions. The first is the vexed question of the definition of markets - the calculation and the relevance of market shares. The second is the appropriate legal and administrative structure for competition policy.

The final section of the chapter introduces the contributed papers. These papers form part of a continuing debate about the economics of market dominance. Many develop in detail points which could only be touched upon in this introductory chapter. More importantly, they serve to demonstrate that this is an area where our knowledge is developing fast, and where dogmatic conclusions should preferably be avoided. They may therefore act as a useful corrective to some of our more categorical statements in this introductory essay.

Economic Analysis of Competition and Monopoly

The prime purpose of competition policy is, in our view, to promote and maintain a process of effective competition so as to achieve a more efficient allocation of resources. Competition policy is often motivated also by other considerations - for example those of political liberty - but in the following we shall focus on the economic criterion of resource allocation. Competition policy cannot properly be viewed in isolation. It should be considered as part of government microeconomic policies generally, including industrial policies, trade policy, regulation, and privatization. This general perspective is needed in order to assess possible conflicts between the instruments of microeconomic policy (see the discussion of innovation below) and to consider which instruments are most appropriate to which targets of policy.

In examining competition policy in these terms we must insist on a broad interpretation of 'resource allocation'. All too often it is seen through the lens of familiar textbook models that are static, and which typically treat the firm as a black box. Recently, however, there have been major advances in our understanding of the *dynamics* of competition, and its role in a world characterized by *imperfect and asymmetric information*. The theory of competition by innovation, which examines the allocation of resources to R & D, is an important example of the dynamic perspective, and we discuss it further below. Other examples of the dynamic approach include analysis of strategic competition (see

Schmalensee's paper in this volume). On imperfect information there now exists a vast literature exploring, for example, *signalling* (in models of product quality, advertising, entry deterrence, etc.), *reputation* (in models of predatory pricing, collusion, etc.), and *incentive systems* (e.g. on the role of competition as an incentive system). Phlips's paper in this volume analyses imperfect information and collusion.

Here is not the place to undertake a survey of these developments. The point is simply that there now exist methods to analyse essential features of competition – of which we have emphasized dynamics and imperfect information – that traditional textbook analyses were not designed to address. These topics have long been recognized as important (consider Schumpeter on innovation) but were not previously so amenable to precise analysis. In the rest of this section we employ these perspectives on competition to examine a range of issues concerned with the economics of market dominance. We consider in turn the *exercise* of dominance, its *acquisition,* and its *maintenance.* These three elements obviously overlap, but it is useful as a starting point to consider them separately. Table 1.1 is a summary chart of the following discussion. It is not intended to be exhaustive. Some aspects of behaviour appear under both the exercise and the maintenance of dominance, for example pricing. This indicates the shortcomings of separating analysis of the two, although that separation is helpful in other respects.

The Exercise of Dominance

Under this heading comes the conduct of firms designed to exploit a position of market dominance, including nonlinear and discriminatory pricing, non-price conditions of sale, advertising, and innovation. These are not the only instruments that may be used in the exercise of dominance, but they are sufficient to illustrate the major points. It hardly needs saying that the same instruments may be used also to acquire or maintain positions of dominance (see below), but it is useful analytically to consider each case separately, even though most real-world situations are hybrid cases.

Traditional analysis focuses on the pricing and output decisions of a dominant firm in a market for a homogeneous good, and shows how a profit-maximizing firm with market power restricts output in order to raise price above marginal cost. Resource allocation becomes distorted from the competitive norm, whose welfare properties are well known. This welfare loss is usually measured by the sum of producers' and consumers' surplus (see Willig, 1976). Using this method, a wide variety of

Table 1.1 Summary chart on dominance

The exercise of dominance	
Price level	Too high
Price discrimination (and related practices)	Likely to be used if possible. Ambiguous welfare effect
Conditions of sale (including vertical restraints)	May be used for pro- or anticompetitive purposes; hence problems of inference
Innovation	Too slow (but competition also has difficulties). Need for suitable industrial policies
Advertising	Too high (but competition also has difficulties)
Brand introduction	Possibly too many
Internal efficiency	Too low; insufficient incentive
The acquisition of dominance	
Government grant	Generalization impossible. For example, patents are usually desirable; regulatory capture is bad
Skill, foresight, and industry	Desirable; to be encouraged
Collusion: explicit ⎤ tacit ⎦	In general bad, but R & D sometimes an exception.
Merger: horizontal	Ambiguous effect on welfare: efficiency gains may offset danger to competition
vertical ⎤ conglomerate ⎦	Neutral for welfare unless part of campaign of predatory conduct
Predatory behaviour	To be condemned, but problems of inference
Maintaining dominance	
Pricing	Low – to discourage entry. Good, unless predatory
Innovation	High, which is usually desirable
Advertising	Probably too high
Brand introduction	Undesirable proliferation

estimates of the social cost of monopoly has been provided, ranging from Harberger's (1954) 0.1 per cent of US GDP to Cowling and Mueller's (1978) estimates in the region of 10 per cent of gross corporate product[1]. One reason why it is important to try to assess the cost of monopoly is that it gives some indication of the possible gains from competition policy. However, social cost should be measured relative to some practically feasible alternative, rather than some theoretical ideal. In this regard, it must be borne in mind that market structure and conduct are in general jointly caused by the fundamental parameters of technology and demand.

The analysis of pricing in markets with differentiated products is less straightforward than the standard homogeneous good case. Demand for the product(s) of a firm then depends to some extent on the prices charged by producers of 'neighbouring' products as well as its own price(s). The question of which product varieties are produced becomes relevant. For example, does the market produce too few or too many varieties? Are they the 'right' ones? What difference does dominance make? Unfortunately, but not surprisingly, there is no simple answer to these questions.

For example, if there are economies of scale there is a trade-off between diversity of choice, which requires more product varieties, and lower unit costs, which require fewer varieties. In general there is no reason to expect market outcomes with product differentiation to be optimal, whatever the market structure, although the direction of inefficiency is typically ambiguous (see Dixit and Stiglitz, 1977; Spence, 1976; Schmalensee, 1978; Salop, 1979).

Although the simplest economic models assume that firms charge uniform prices for their products, it commonly happens that price is made contingent upon, for example, quantity purchased, or the time or place of purchase. In addition, conditions of sale ('vertical restraints') are often imposed upon the buyer, especially in transactions between manufacturers and retailers. These questions of discriminatory pricing and conditions of sale have often been the subject of antitrust scrutiny. As regards the economic analysis of these practices, there are two distinct questions. First, there is the issue of whether the practices are detrimental to competition, or to social welfare generally. Secondly, there is the issue

---

[1] Littlechild (1981) criticized Cowling and Mueller's calculations, and they (1981) replied to him. Kay (1983) analyses the social cost of monopoly in a general (rather than partial) equilibrium framework. The social cost of oligopoly and the value of competition is investigated by Masson and Shaanan (1984).

of whether the practices are indicative of a lack of effective competition.

A thorough overview of the literature on price discrimination, including nonlinear pricing, is provided by Phlips (1983). Contrary to what is often believed, optimal resource allocation generally requires discriminatory pricing. However, it is another question whether it is desirable for a dominant firm to be able to practise price discriminations. For example, Schmalensee (1981a) shows that simple price discrimination is undesirable unless it leads to higher output, because discrimination allocates output across consumers inefficiently, which is undesirable unless offset by higher total output. The latter condition may be met in so far as price discrimination serves to open up new markets. (For analyses of nonlinear pricing see Oi (1971), Schmalensee (1981b), and Maskin and Riley (1984).) A form of nonlinear pricing occurs where price is related to a consumer's *past* purchases from the supplier. This 'loyalty rebate' form of quantity discount gives rise to switching costs, because the discount is lost by a consumer who changes supplier. Airline discounts for frequent fliers are an example. Klemperer (1984) shows how switching costs may facilitate collusion and entry deterrence. (See also von Weizsäcker (1984).)

A form of nonlinear pricing by multiproduct firms is commodity bundling – the practice of selling several goods as a package. Bundling allegations have of course been central to major antitrust cases, such as those involving IBM. One rationale for bundling is to economize on the costs of production and exchange, but there also exists another explanation which is related to price discrimination. Adams and Yellen (1976) show how bundling can serve to sort consumers into groups with different demand characteristics and thereby enhance profits.

In addition to welfare questions concerning price discrimination, there is the positive question of whether competition eliminates the practice. In that event the existence of discrimination would be indicative of market power. Questions of this sort must be addressed if dominance is to be inferred from allegedly abusive conduct. Neven and Phlips (1985) show that price discrimination can occur in oligopoly, and they apply their results to the European car market, in which substantial international price differences have existed. In their model discrimination vanishes as competition grows. Oren et al. (1983) examine competitive nonlinear pricing. They show that price approaches marginal cost as the number of firms grows. However, Katz (1984a) has a model with informed and uninformed consumers in which price discrimination does occur at (monopolistically) competitive equilibrium.

We now turn to other conditions of sale. Manufacturers sometimes place vertical restraints on their retailers, including exclusive dealing conditions and territorial allocation. A type of vertical restraint which is illegal in many jurisdictions is resale price maintenance (RPM). Hay (1985a) distinguishes between vertical restraints which affect competition with other brands (*inter*brand competition), and those which affect competition between retailers of the brand in question (*intra*brand competition). The latter type of restraint has been the subject of much recent controversy. Restraints imposed by a manufacturer upon competition between retailers of his product should not be treated on a par with horizontal agreement between the retailers. The difference is that it is the manufacturer who places the restraint, and *prima facie* he has no incentive to see his retailers collude. (On the other hand he may be acting at the behest of the retailers, or with a view to facilitating collusion with other manufacturers, both of which would be undesirable.) Telser (1960) considered vertical restraints upon intrabrand competition as a way round the free-rider problem between retailers that exists when they provide desirable pre-sales services for which it is impossible to charge. (Each would prefer to benefit from the services provided by other retailers rather than provide his own.) On this view, such vertical restraints enhance efficiency and competition ·between brands. Recent elaborations of this idea have been made by Mathewson and Winter (1984) and Marvel and McCafferty (1984).

Here there is an obvious difficulty of distinguishing between the pro- and anticompetitive explanations of the phenomenon in particular cases. Antitrust policy has often been hostile to vertical restraints, despite their possible benefits. However, in the United States a somewhat more permissive attitude towards intrabrand vertical restraints has recently been adopted (for example in the Vertical Restraint Guidelines issued by the Department of Justice; see Hay's paper in this volume). Vertical restraints involving price continue to be *per se* unlawful, but a rule of reason approach is followed for non-price restraints. Economic analysis supports this step in respect of non-price vertical restraints on intrabrand competition, and would justify a similar approach for vertical restraints involving price.

Having considered pricing and conditions of sale, we now turn to other aspects of company behaviour. A welfare analysis of *advertising* is given by Dixit and Norman (1978). They focus on advertising which changes tastes (as opposed to the role of advertising as a signal of quality in a world of imperfect information: see Nelson, 1970; Milgrom and

Roberts, 1984). A difficulty here is that the welfare yardstick – consumer tastes – is itself altered by the conduct being assessed. Dixit and Norman nevertheless find that the market equilibrium level of advertising is socially excessive even when judged by post-advertising tastes. The result holds for a variety of market structures; indeed it holds more strongly in monopolistic competition or oligopoly than in monopoly. Non-price competition in the form of advertising can be especially wasteful.

The relationship between *innovation* and market structure is one of even greater complexity. Intuitively one might expect that a monopolist would introduce new products and processes too slowly. As Hicks said, perhaps the greatest monopoly profit is the quiet life. And indeed, it can be shown that a profit-maximizing monopolist's incentive to introduce a new technology is smaller than its value to society. The comparison between alternative market structures again yields ambiguous results (and may be inappropriate if market structure is endogenous: see Dasgupta and Stiglitz, 1980). A central difficulty is the appropriability problem. An incentive to make the next innovation requires that the innovator be protected from immediate imitation by rivals, but an innovation is most efficiently exploited when it is freely available, in which case the innovator receives no reward unless there are subsidies to R & D. Von Weizsäcker's (1980) schema of different levels of competition makes the point clearly: proper incentives for competition by innovation require restrictions on competition in product markets, in combination with other policy measures.

Whereas the appropriability problem leads to the expectation that each firm does *too little* R & D, there may also exist excessive duplication of R & D effort if each firm is attempting to do essentially the same thing. In the aggregate it is therefore possible that *more* R & D expenditure occurs than is socially optimal (see Dasgupta and Stiglitz, 1980 for an illustration). The effect on welfare of increased competition, in the sense of more firms competing, is ambiguous. The competition will be beneficial in the product market, where the price-cost wedge will narrow but the allocation of resources to R & D may conceivably worsen, either because incentives to do R & D are dulled when there are problems of appropriability, or because of increased duplication of research efforts. And we have yet to consider innovation in the presence of entry threats (see below).

Innovation is perhaps the clearest example in which competition policy must be considered as part of microeconomic policies more generally. On the one hand, competition policy in innovative industries cannot ignore its consequences for the allocation of resources to R & D. And on the other hand it must be seen as one policy among several, including patent and copyright laws, R & D subsidies, R & D licensing policies, and other instruments of industrial policy. A number of recent antitrust cases, which we shall refer to below, concern just these questions. (On R & D joint ventures, licensing arrangements, and mergers in high-technology industries, see Katz (1989), Shapiro (1985), and Ordover and Willig (1985).)

Until now we have assumed implicitly that a firm is a profit-maximizing black box, but dominance is ultimately exercised by decision-takers within firms, namely managers, whose interests may not lie with maximum profits. The internal efficiency of a firm depends on the degree of competition it faces in so far as competition affects managerial incentives and opportunities (recall Hicks's remark about the quiet life). One way in which competition sharpens incentives, and hence internal efficiency, is by permitting the *relative* performance of agents to be compared. When such comparisons can be made, rewards naturally become linked – implicitly if not explicitly – to relative performance. This idea is related to Leibenstein's well-known (1966) paper on X-efficiency, where it was argued that the welfare loss to society due to X-inefficiency within firms outweighed that due to inefficient resource allocation in the markets, and also that competition spurs X-efficiency. The role of competition as an incentive mechanism is an important part of any welfare analysis of competition and monopoly.

To summarize this section on the exercise of monopoly, we have seen that the non-price decisions of managers in a dominant firm are just as likely to be out of line with the public interest as their pricing decisions. Relative to the 'first best' there is, for example, a tendency to excessive advertising, insufficient innovation, and internal inefficiency. However, comparison with the first best is not entirely appropriate if firms are to be left to take their decisions independently. In that event the proper comparison is between alternative market outcomes, rather than between some market outcome and the 'social optimum'.

The Acquisition of Dominance

If the exercise of dominance tends to be to the detriment of consumers, there is a *prima facie* case for policy to prevent the achievement of domi-nant positions. However, market power can be acquired in a variety of ways, of which we shall focus on five:

The grant of market power by public authority
Skill, foresight, and industry
Collusion
Merger
Predatory behaviour

The grant of market power by public authority   Firms in the utility industries (power, water, and telecommunications) and elsewhere have
often enjoyed monopoly franchises granted by government. In the
United States, private firms have operated in those industries subject to a
framework of regulation. In other countries, for example the UK, the
utilities have generally been in public ownership and operated according
to economic, financial, and other criteria of a loosely specified nature.
Many of these industries (or parts of them) are or have been natural
monopolies, i.e. efficiency requires single-firm production.

Numerous criticisms have been levelled against US-style regulation.
Regulatory systems, even when operated by benign and omniscient agencies, can give rise to major inefficiencies in resource allocation, as the
literature on Averch-Johnson effects, rate-base padding and gold-plating
makes clear (see Kahn, 1971; Baumol and Klevorick, 1970).

If regulators are human, however, matters may be even worse. The so-
called 'economic' theory of regulation – or 'capture' theory – describes
how regulatory agencies may end up more or less in the pockets of those
whom they purport to regulate (see Stigler, 1971; Posner, 1974; and
Brock's 1981 account of the US telecommunications industry). In
response to these perceived failings, there has been a substantial
dismantling of regulation in a number of American industries. In the last
decade or so deregulation has occurred in airlines, trucking, financial
services, and telecommunications, to name a few. The massive re-
organization of the telecommunications industry followed the ending of
the case against AT & T in January 1982. The company was divested of its
various local operating companies (horizontal separation) but retained its
long-distance, manufacturing, and research divisions (vertical
integration). Public authority has thereby rescinded much of its earlier
grant of market power, and regulation has been partly replaced by
monitoring by antitrust authorities.

In the UK several major nationalized industries – many of them with
substantial market power – are being transferred to private ownership.
The main examples include telecommunications, gas, water, airports,
and possibly electricity. Regulatory bodies are being established, and
competition is being introduced on a limited scale. Criticisms have

been made that the liberalizing measures introduced by governments stop a long way short of what could and should have been achieved (see Vickers and Yarrow, 1985). The privatization of utility companies in the UK is happening in a way that effectively involves government grant of market power. We comment further on this below.

Skill, foresight, and industry   The fact that a firm might owe its position of market power to competitive superiority over its rivals – to 'skill, foresight, and industry' as it was put in the Alcoa case (see later) – poses a dilemma for antitrust policy. Even if it could be shown unequivocally that dominance was bad, a universal condemnation of dominance would stifle competition *for* positions of market power, which could be detrimental in overall terms. Patents provide the clearest example. The results accruing from market power due to the ownership of a patent are of course the very reason why firms compete by innovation for the patent. To diminish that market power is to diminish the incentive to innovate. The same applies to firms that owe their positions of market strength to superior organizational efficiency, marketing strategies, and so on. To attack their competitive success would be to subvert the process itself.

There are two principal difficulties. The first is to strike a balance between the welfare gain of dynamic competition and the welfare loss of the resulting market power. This balance depends on such things as the length of patent life, and also upon the stance adopted by antitrust authorities towards firms that appear to owe their success partly to superior skill, foresight, and industry. The second difficulty is that of inferring the cause of a firm's market position. Does IBM owe its position to succeeding in fair competition with others, or to anticompetitive practices? We discuss further this problem of inference, and the inevitable errors to which it leads, in a later section on the economics of policy.

Collusion   Collusion may be thought of as multifirm dominance. Such dominance is gained by the explicit or tacit co-ordination of firms' strategies. With few exceptions, explicit horizontal agreements between firms are banned. Research joint ventures are a type of horizontal agreement that is sometimes permitted – partly to avoid excessive duplication of R & D efforts and also perhaps for international strategic reasons. Cartels do of course have their defenders, often from the industries in question, who appeal to such things as rationalization, risk reduction, and forward planning. Aside from the area of R & D, where special considerations apply, defences of this sort are generally unimpressive and not such as to disturb the case for the *per se* condemnation of explicit horizontal agreements that exists under most jurisdictions.

Tacit collusion poses particular problems. There is no reason to suppose that the pursuit of self-interest by firms will necessarily undermine tacit collusion. Indeed, it has been shown rigorously, and under a variety of assumptions about information conditions, that collusive outcomes are supportable as Nash (and perfect) equilibria in repeated games (see Friedman, 1971; Abreu, 1984; Kreps et al., 1982; Green and Porter, 1984). That is to say, collusive outcomes can perfectly well occur as a result of the independent pursuit of each firm's self-interest. Collusion is maintained by the (credible) threat of retaliation in the event of defection. The range of threat strategies available – and hence the range of supportable collusive outcomes – depends on the information conditions and incentive structures of each firm. Although it is difficult for public policy to strike directly at tacit collusion (after all, each firm is behaving independently) it can affect the information and incentive conditions that are more or less conducive to collusion. For example, information agreements have long been a target of antitrust scrutiny, because there is more incentive for one firm to 'cheat' if it is more difficult for others to detect that cheating.

Similarly, there is also a role for public policy to attack 'facilitating practices' which create incentive structures conducive to collusion. Salop (1985) shows how pricing systems involving 'most favoured nation' clauses or 'meeting competition clauses' may facilitate collusion.

While we favour policy against facilitating practices, it is only a partial answer to the problem of multifirm dominance. Existing antitrust policies contain weaknesses in this regard, although it is no easy matter to see what practicable policies and remedies could be designed to combat tacit collusion (see Phlips's paper in this volume).

Merger   Much of the increase in industrial concentration to have occurred in recent decades is due to horizontal merger (see Hannah and Kay, 1977, for evidence on the UK). Although concentration and market power are by no means the same, merger is unquestionably one of the main possible routes to a dominant position. Superficially, merger might appear to be the ultimate form of explicit collusion, and it may be asked why the prohibition of the latter does not extend to the former. There are two reasons. The first is that merger can yield efficiency gains, for example if there are scale economies (see Williamson, 1968). The realization of those gains could offset welfare losses due to reduced competition. The second reason is that the threat of takeover in principle operates as a discipline on managerial behaviour: in a world where ownership and control are divorced, and where shareholdings are typically dispersed, the threat of shareholder revolt is as nothing compared with the takeover threat. The takeover system therefore permits a 'market for control' (see Manne, 1965; Grossman and Hart, 1980; Yarrow, 1985). An outright condemnation of mergers would therefore be inappropriate.

But how are the pros and cons of a merger to be weighed up? The question, in our view, is largely one of the burden of proof. We contend that, where a merger is likely to reduce competition, the burden of proof should lie with the firm(s) proposing merger. This is for three reasons. The first is that the firm stands to gain from *both* the gain in efficiency and the reduction of competition, whereas the merger's effects on welfare generally are ambiguous. The second reason is that *experience* of horizontal mergers is disappointing even when measured by the yardstick of firms' profitability (see Meeks, 1977; Firth, 1979). Moreover, the disappointing profit performance of merger perhaps suggests that they are motivated more by managerial motives (size, growth, prestige, defence against being taken over) than by efficiency considerations. This goes against the incentive argument for the takeover system. Our third reason is the vast asymmetry of information that exists as between parties to a merger and the competition authorities. In sum, the fact that those favouring the merger have a greater incentive and more information than the authorities, together with the historical experience just described, add up to a strong case for placing the burden of proof on them. We return to this point later, in our discussion of the economics of policy.

Finally we must mention vertical and conglomerate mergers. It is not evident how such mergers, in themselves, pose a serious threat to competition. Upstream vertical merger might be used to pre-empt supplies to horizontal competitors, and conglomerate merger might yield financial strength such as to enable predatory behaviour. But what is undesirable in these examples is not merger *per se*, but the accompanying anticompetitive conduct. In principle it would be better to strike at that conduct directly rather than to condemn the mergers which might have some beneficial consequences. But the practical problems of identifying predatory behaviour (see below) are such that in some cases it would be better to remove the temptation by disallowing the merger.

Predatory behaviour   The final route to dominance that we consider is predatory behaviour designed to drive existing competitors from the market. Celebrated antitrust cases – such as Standard Oil – have involved allegations of such conduct. Predatory conduct is usually considered in relation to the driving out of new entrants, rather than already existing rivals, in which case it comes under the heading of 'maintaining dominance'; and indeed we shall discuss it there. However, it is also a possible way of gaining a dominant position in the first place, or at any rate of strengthening a market position acquired by other means.

Maintaining Dominance

Potential competition from the entry and expansion of rival firms has always been regarded in industrial organization as the main market mechanism for counteracting the adverse effects of dominance. The idea is that dominance would rapidly be eroded by those competitors if the dominant firm(s) became inefficient or inattentive to consumers' wishes. Therefore the threat of potential competition, and its attendant penalties, constrain the firm not to abuse its market position. Indeed, that position is hardly one of market power if potential competition is strong.

The theory of contestable markets (see Baumol, 1982; Baumol et al., 1982) states this point in its purest form. A contestable market is one where existing firms are completely vulnerable to hit-and-run entry: cost conditions are the same for all firms; there are no sunk costs of entry (so exit is costless); and entry can occur successfully before existing firms have time to respond. Market performance is optimal, subject to the constraint that firms make non-negative profits. This is so irrespective of the observed market structure, which is anyway determined by fundamental cost and demand conditions. The authors of the theory argue that it offers a more useful notion of a 'competitive' market than the textbook model of perfect competition in which there is a vast number of small firms in the market. Entry conditions, rather than concentration levels, are what matter, and market structure is endogenous. Contestability theory has been the subject of much critical discussion (see Brock, 1983; Spence, 1983; Schwartz and Reynolds, 1983; and Shepherd, 1984). It has been questioned whether a contestable market does provide an appropriate benchmark for assessing market structure, on the grounds that the assumptions that imply vulnerability to hit-and-run entry are both implausible and non-robust to small variations. Contestability theory has nevertheless underlined the importance of assumptions about sunk costs in the analysis of entry conditions.

While contestability theory assumes that sunk costs do not exist, another branch of the literature – on strategic entry deterrence – has explored how they may be used to maintain positions of market dominance. The simple schema in figure 1.1 illustrates this idea. The game depicted below has two stages. First, the incumbent dominant firm commits expenditures on some 'strategic variable' K, which may be thought of as capacity, advertising, or R & D, for example. This affects the payoff that the rival would receive if it entered the market, and so it affects the entry decision. In this framework, strategic entry deterrence consists in choosing a level of K such that the expected payoff to an entrant, $R^E(K)$, would be less than zero. It is vital that the choice of K be sunk or irreversible; otherwise it would be 'undone' in the event of entry and so would not affect the entrant's decision. Sunk costs for the entrant are also necessary for $R^E(K)$ to be depressed below zero.

The dominant firm's choice of strategic variable could affect the rival's perception of post-entry profitability in a number of ways. In particular, it could influence

1 The incumbent's costs – as with R & D;
2 The costs of both firms – as with wage deals;
3 The opportunities of the rival – as with pre-emptive patenting;
4 Market demand conditions – as with advertising or brand proliferation;
5 The rival's belief about the incumbent – as with signalling costs by pre-entry pricing or by gaining a reputation by predatory pricing.

References to this literature may be found in Schmalensee's paper in this volume, Geroski and Jacquemin (1984), and Vickers (1985).

What are the consequences for welfare of maintaining dominance by strategic entry deterrence? As might be expected, there exists no general answer to this question. Consider, for example, strategic entry deterrence by investment in capital which lowers the incumbent's cost level. Once entry has been deterred, the incumbent might produce his output inefficiently because he has committed himself to a capital-intensive mode of production. But against this productive inefficiency must be set the gain in allocative efficiency arising from the larger output supplied by the firm due to its costs being lower than they would otherwise be. Moreover,

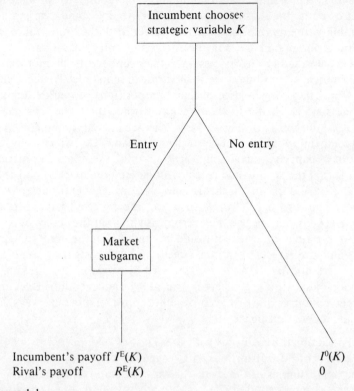

Incumbent's payoff $I^E(K)$ $I^0(K)$
Rival's payoff $R^E(K)$ 0

Figure 1.1

actual entry may or may not be desirable. It will tend to lower price, but might also involve high fixed costs being incurred. More generally it is interesting to compare *three* alternatives:

a   The outcome with strategic entry deterrence;
b   The outcome with no strategic entry deterrence (and hence with entry);
c   The outcome when there is no entry threat in the first place.

By (b) we mean the situation in which the incumbent behaves non-strategically, i.e. as if there were no entry threat.

The comparison between (a) and (c) has to do with the value of the entry *threat*. That threat can have the disadvantage of inducing unproductive activities designed to deter entry, but it can also act as a spur to efficiency and innovation. Recall that earlier it was stated that a

dominant firm not faced with entry threats would innovate too slowly
from a social point of view. That tendency is offset by entry threats in so
far as they induce extra innovative efforts from the dominant firm. An
important point is that the value of the threat is likely to depend on the
effectiveness of policies against anticompetitive prices.

Although unambiguous welfare results of a general kind are not to be
had, and the particular circumstances of each case therefore matter, we
would say that existing theory and evidence suggests that the ranking of
the three situations discussed would typically be (b), (a), (c). That is to
say, we believe that entry threats are usually desirable (even if entry does
not actually occur) and that strategic entry deterrence (for example by
anticompetitive practices) is usually undesirable. In some circumstances
the ordering would be different, but the presumption should be in favour
of free entry and against the various strategies devised by dominant firms
to deter entry. The onus of proof, in our view, should be on those
seeking to show otherwise.

We conclude this section on maintaining dominance by stating a fundamental difficulty for antitrust policy in this area. It is the problem of
distinguishing between anticompetitive business practices whose object is
to maintain dominance, and procompetitive business practices which are
impelled by the competitive process itself. Nowhere is this difficulty
more apparent than with allegedly predatory pricing. Aggressive pricing
is after all what the competitive process should bring about; on the other
hand it may subvert the process itself. The cost of an excessively tough
policy against possibly predatory pricing is that it may deny consumers
the benefits of the competition that it was intended to promote. The
same danger exists with respect to other means of maintaining dominance, for example by 'predatory' innovation. The next section on the
economics of policy takes up this theme.

The Economics of Policy

It would be too hasty to jump from the foregoing theoretical analysis to a
consideration of policy in practice without first discussing what may be
termed 'the economics of policy'. By this we mean the balancing of the
costs and possible benefits of various types of policy measure. In practice
the policy-maker obviously has neither the powers nor the information to
bring about the optimal outcome in a particular industry (whatever
that may be). Indeed, it is an essential part of the market system that
the *decentralized* decisions of independent firms, mediated by the

competitive process, determine the allocation of resources. Though imperfect, the competitive mechanism has more or less desirable properties. The question for policy, then, is how best to promote and maintain the *process* of effective competition, with a view to inducing a more efficient allocation of resources. Competition policy should be seen, along with other instruments of microeconomic policy, as part of the rules of the game in which firms operate. Its influence is indirect, and operates via its effect on the incentives and opportunities of decision-makers within firms.

We saw in the previous section that the effects of competition and of policy measures upon welfare are often ambiguous. That is to say, it is not possible to deduce clear-cut results by theorizing from an armchair; the facts matter, entirely as one would expect. However, when one considers the appropriate design of policy, it is quite unsatisfactory to say that 'it all depends on the particular circumstances at hand, and every case must therefore be investigated in detail on its merits.' For competition policy is costly to administer, and the costs of in-depth investigations of every case would outweigh the likely gains. Policy therefore needs to contain a set of rules and presumptions that cut short more detailed examinations where it is appropriate to do so. Quite apart from being essential to the containing of administration (and other) costs, such rules and presumptions have the added advantage of enhancing the predictability of policy.

This question of the appropriate balance between 'rules' and 'discretion' is essentially one of how much information to acquire about a particular case before deciding it. The more information a decision-maker has, the better his decision is likely to be. Since his information is inevitably imperfect, mistakes are bound to be made. There is the risk of condemning or discouraging desirable behaviour (a 'type I' error) and the risk of permitting or promoting undesirable behaviour (a 'type II error'; see Hay, 1981).

The value of additional information depends upon how much it reduces the chance of a wrong decision and upon the importance of the particular case. For example, it makes sense to have a rule against cartel pricing agreements that is not contingent upon the particular circumstances at hand, because, even if one or two such agreements might conceivably be in the public interest, hardly any decisions would be altered in the light of the information gained from detailed investigations, and the latter would be costly. As to the size or importance of particular cases, it is obviously sensible, other things being equal, to investigate those cases where the effect on the public interest is larger rather than smaller; then the likely return on investment in antitrust is maximized. Obvious though this principle may seem, the selection of cases for antitrust scrutiny has not always accorded with it.

In the rest of this section we state briefly our own views on appropriate policy towards the market dominance questions considered in the previous section. We consider in turn the acquisition, maintenance, and exercise of dominance. Our views reflect the following general principles. First, policy should be framed with a view to minimizing the cost of the two types of error (condemning desirable behaviour and permitting undesirable behaviour) together with the costs of administering policy. Fine-tuning being impossible, some rules and guidelines are necessary. But in major cases, where welfare implications are large, detailed investigations are called for.

Secondly, we believe that, although competitive outcomes cannot be demonstrated to be preferable in all possible circumstances, the process of effective competition is by and large the most practicable system for achieving more efficient resource allocation (in the broad sense that includes static, dynamic, and internal efficiency). The principal concern of competition policy should therefore be the promotion and maintenance of the process of effective competition. However, that should not be the only concern of competition policy, because in some cases it might be possible to show that the diminution of competition (due, say, to a merger) is outweighed by other advantages (e.g. scale economies). Those considerations should sometimes be taken into account, but the onus of proof should lie with those contending that the diminution of competition is outweighed by the other factors.

Thirdly, we believe that it would be wrong to condemn allegedly anti-competitive conduct without reason to believe that effective competition is absent (or would be absent if the conduct were permitted). This does not imply that other microeconomic policies should not apply. For example, industrial policies to promote innovation might be eminently suitable in a competitive environment.

Finally, as with crime, preventing dominance is better than curing it. This has implications for mergers and privatization policies. Of course it is often too late for prevention, and remedies must be applied. In extreme cases regulation is appropriate, despite its well-known drawbacks. In such cases it still makes sense to minimize the burden of regulation by promoting effective competition in every feasible way.

Policies toward the Acquisition of Dominance

In the previous section we considered five ways of acquiring a dominant position: government grant; skill, foresight, and industry; collusion; merger; and predatory behaviour. Given the undesirability of the exercise of dominance, together with the difficulties of curbing existing market power, it naturally makes sense to seek to prevent firms from acquiring dominance. The problem is, however, that some of the routes to dominance are more benign than others, but it is not always easy to determine the causes of a particular position of market power. Policy must avoid being so fierce as to discourage skill, foresight, and industry, at the same time as avoiding such laxity as to permit the unchecked accumulation of market power by anticompetitive means.

As regards the grant of a dominant position by public authority, two broad cases must be distinguished. First, there is the case where fundamental cost and demand conditions make it inevitable that a dominant position will exist. Then it is essential to regulate in some form or other, and public ownership may be appropriate. However, even in this case – and irrespective of whether ownership is public or private – it is important to promote competition wherever possible. The second case is where there is scope for competitive forces to operate. Then the grant of a dominant position is unnecessary, and every step should be taken to give full rein to competitive forces, for example by introducing effective liberalization. In that way the extent of market power is minimized, and the burden of regulation is lessened.

Deregulation in the United States has involved the promotion of competition in industries where legal and regulatory impediments to competition previously existed. In short, the grant of market power by public authority has been rescinded. In the privatization programme in the UK, positions of market power that were in public ownership are being transferred into private hands. This transfer is being accompanied by some measures to promote competition, but these fall a long way short of what might have been accomplished, and the resulting strain on the new regulatory authorities is considerable.

As regards the acquisition of dominance by skill, foresight, and industry, the fundamental problem is to strike a balance between the dynamic advantages of encouraging innovation and efficiency (in the broad sense) and the disadvantages of the dominant positions that may result from that dynamic competition. This tension has been central to numerous celebrated antitrust cases, such as those involving Xerox,

Kodak, and IBM. In principle it is of course quite wrong to deprive the winners of genuine dynamic competition of the fruits of their success, but the practical problem is to distinguish between fair and foul competitive success. This problem of inference is well illustrated by predatory pricing, which we consider further below.

As to the gaining of market power by collusion, the *per se* illegality of explicit price-fixing agreements is required. Agreements regarding non-price behaviour should generally be condemned, but R & D agreements are a possible exception, as was discussed above. Tacit collusion may be similar in effect to explicit collusion, but is much harder to legislate against. Nevertheless we believe that policy can do two things. First, it can attempt to remove preconditions that are conducive to implicit collusion by condemning various types of information agreement and other facilitating practices (see Salop, 1985; and Phlips's paper in this volume). Secondly, where it is quite plain that competition is ineffective in an oligopolistic industry, a (multifirm) monopoly case should be brought. We have in mind cases of large persistent price differentials between similar markets, which could not last if competition were effective. Here it would perhaps be wrong to penalize the firms involved by fining them, since each is pursuing its own interests independently. This notion of 'no fault liability' was much discussed in the United States in the 1970s but has not been implemented.

Merger is the most obvious route to dominance, and merger policy is the most systematic branch of policy against its acquisition. However, some mergers may be desirable in so far as they lead to efficiency gains, and it can be argued that the takeover system in general has the merit of enhancing internal efficiency by making a market for corporate control (although the empirical evidence suggests that efficiency gains from merger are disappointing). Therefore it would be wrong to condemn mergers in the same way as explicit agreements between firms. The schema in figure 1.2 summarizes our own view on appropriate mergers policy.

The schema incorporates some of the general remarks made earlier. The merger should be subject to investigation only if *prima facie* it appears that it might jeopardize competition. If it is found not to threaten competition, it should be allowed. Otherwise it should be condemned unless the case can be proven that countervailing benefits are likely to flow from the merger. In short, competition should be the prime consideration, and the onus of proof should lie with those who seek to argue otherwise.

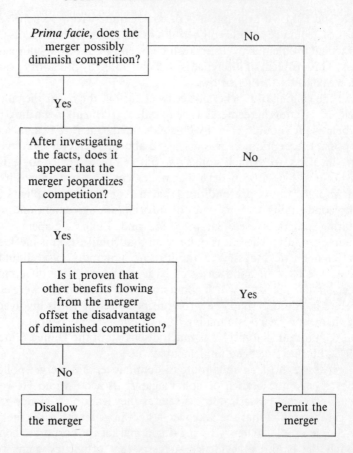

Figure 1.2

Horizontal mergers are in general more threatening to effective competition than vertical or conglomerate mergers, and we favour a correspondingly tougher policy towards them. Vertical merger can jeopardize competition if, for example, it results in competitors being denied inputs or outlets on fair terms. It might be said that policy on anticompetitive conduct, rather than merger policy, is the appropriate tool to deal with such situations, but we do not entirely agree. Given that a perfect and costless policy against anticompetitive practices is not possible, it is sometimes appropriate to use vertical merger policy to prevent the incentive and opportunity for the exclusionary conduct just mentioned. It is also conceivable that a conglomerate merger could be anticompetitive in as much as it enables predatory conduct to be financed, but in general we see no need to subject conglomerate mergers to antitrust scrutiny.

The acquisition of dominance by predatory means is perhaps the most difficult case for policy. There are two types of evidence of predatory behaviour – evidence of predatory intent, and the conduct itself. It is notoriously difficult to assess evidence regarding intent. On the one hand, a predator would take great care to ensure that company files – especially at senior levels – were purged of material suggesting predatory intent. On the other hand, documentary evidence of the desire of (say) the marketing department to fight hard against competitors so as to take their business might indicate no more than (pro)competitive zeal. This is not to say that all evidence on intent is worthless, but it does suggest that the allegedly predatory conduct will be central to any investigation.

However, there are also formidable difficulties of distinguishing between pro- and anticompetitive conduct, because in the short run they share the same outward appearance – low prices, new products, and so on. The clearest instances of predatory pricing are caught by the cost-based rule proposed by Areeda and Turner (1975), but it has been criticized for being too permissive and for neglecting dynamic and strategic factors (see Hay, 1981 for a review of the debate). In the longer term, it may be somewhat easier to distinguish between pro- and anticompetitive pricing. The latter would be associated with exit of rivals followed by a reversion to higher prices. Such a pattern of events would be strongly suggestive – though perhaps not absolute proof – of predatory behaviour, and should be met by antitrust remedies unless the firm can account for its behaviour in procompetitive terms. One remedy would be to require that the lower price level be maintained for a period, but a *rule* to that effect would be too mechanistic; other remedies might be more suitable in particular cases.

Recent analyses of strategic commitment show that *non*-price predation may be as much of a problem as predatory pricing (see for example, Salop, 1981, which contains several examinations of non-price predatory behaviour including case studies). But although recent work on the economics of predatory practices has greatly improved methods for analysing particular cases, it has not delivered *general* rules applicable to all types of industry. This simply reflects the heterogeneity of industries. Therefore it has to be concluded that there are no short cuts to solving the problem of policy regarding predatory practices. Rules such as that proposed by Areeda and Turner go some way, but there remains the need for detailed investigations of possibly predatory behaviour in major cases.

Policies towards the Maintenance of Dominance

To maintain a dominant position it is essential to limit the entry and growth of rival firms. When freedom of entry exists, the entry and growth of rivals is prevented only if existing firms meet consumers' wishes efficiently (whatever market shares may be). When freedom of entry does not exist, it is useful to employ Salop's (1979) distinction between innocent and strategic barriers to entry. Innocent barriers exist irrespective of the behaviour of existing firms. Policy against predatory behaviour is of no consequence in such cases, and other remedies must be sought (see the following subsection). Strategic entry barriers, on the other hand, are deliberately created by existing firms to make entry unattractive. Strategic entry deterrence is related to *sunk costs* in two ways. First, the presence of sunk costs implies that the industry is not vulnerable to hit-and-run entry (Baumol, 1982). Secondly, the sinking of costs can create credible threats to respond aggressively to entry.

Policy can influence barriers to entry – and hence the ease of maintaining dominance – in two principal ways. First, legal measures can affect entry conditions. For example, legislation on patents, copyrights and registered designs imposes restrictions on entry that are on the whole desirable. The requirement that firms in an industry be licensed or authorized can be another barrier to entry, depending on the liberality of licensing policy. Deregulation in the United States has involved the lifting of various types of entry restriction, and its impact – in airlines, trucking, telecommunications, and so on – has been very considerable (see Bailey, 1986). Secondly, policy can influence strategic entry barriers by affecting the conduct of existing firms. The threat of predatory pricing, if credible, is a classic strategic entry deterrent, and an effective policy against predatory practices is therefore an essential part of measures to liberalize entry conditions. The legal possibility of entry does not imply the effectiveness of entry threats unless predation is checked. Policy on industry structure, as well as towards conduct, can affect the likelihood of predatory behaviour. For example, a vertically integrated firm with a dominant position upstream in an industry may be able to use that position to thwart competition downstream. If it is impossible to undo its upstream dominance, a case may exist for separating the firm's upstream and downstream operations so as to permit competition downstream. However, vertical separation is but one solution to the problem, and measures affecting the upstream pricing might offer a more attractive alternative.

In summary, the best antidote to firms' behaviour designed to maintain positions of dominance is to promote the freedom of entry. That requires not only the lifting of restrictions on entry, but also tough measures against strategic behaviour intended to thwart entry. When entry threats are effective, the only way for a firm to maintain its market position is by meeting consumers' demands efficiently. Such a position is not one of dominance in any reasonable sense.

Policies towards the Exercise of Dominance

In the previous section we discussed how the business practices of dominant firms are unlikely to accord with efficient resource allocation. In particular we considered pricing policies, other conditions of sale, innovation, advertising, brand introduction, and internal efficiency. Once a position of market dominance has been acquired, what practical policy measures are appropriate to the problem of the exercise of dominance?

The answer to this question depends first upon how the position of dominance was acquired. If its cause was skill, foresight, and industry, then it would be a subversion of the process of (dynamic) competition to intervene to deny the firm the market position that it has won by lawful and desirable means. If the dominant position is due to other causes, the next question is whether it is possible and desirable to introduce effective competition. In the previous subsection we discussed measures to promote and maintain liberal entry conditions.

An alternative (or addition) to the promotion of entry is the dissolution of the dominant firm – an extreme remedy, but one that has been used on occasions (for example with Standard Oil). However, this policy may not be desirable when the dominant position is called for by underlying cost and demand conditions – as with natural monopoly, for example. Dissolution might then imply the loss of substantial economies of scale or scope. In those circumstances it is more appropriate to deal with industry conduct rather than industry structure, since structure is determined endogenously by given fundamental conditions.

We have already discussed policy towards firms' conduct in relation to the acquisition and maintenance of dominance. However, when there exists no feasible prospect of competition, different issues arise. Essentially we are left with forms of policy ranging from full-scale regulation of the public utility type to the prohibition of the particular business practices of a firm. No form of regulation is without cost, and this cost must naturally be considered in relation to the potential gains to be had from regulation. The latter depend on the size and importance of the industry, and upon the scope for raising price above cost (if the monopoly price barely covers cost there is less need for regulation). Several aspects of conduct may be subject to regulation, including pricing, quality, and other non-price behaviour.

As regards the regulation of pricing where competition is infeasible, we believe that there is merit in the $RPI-X$ scheme being adopted in the UK towards the privatized utility companies, *provided that* X is set appropriately and that there are quality safeguards. That scheme constrains the dominant firm to keep the annual increase in the price of its services below the inflation rate minus X per cent. The merit of the scheme is that, in the short run, it gives the firm the right incentives for cost reduction. However, the pricing formula is revised periodically, and in the longer run it is therefore impossible to exclude some incentives for strategic behaviour in relation to costs, and the attendant drawbacks of rate-of-return regulation. This danger is minimized when the regulatory body is well informed as to the potential cost reductions available, and especially when comparisons between firms (e.g. between regional units) are available. Another danger is that if $RPI-X$ is applied to an index of the firm's products, the firm may be able to exploit its market power by altering relative prices within the index. Safeguards against such behaviour are required.

As to other aspects of pricing behaviour, we explained above that there are few unambiguous welfare results – for example concerning price discrimination (in its various forms). Nevertheless there is a case for a rebuttable presumption against simple price discrimination, where it is unrelated to cost differences. More complex forms of price discrimination (e.g. basing price on time or place) are another matter. These are common, and desirable, in many utility industries, where there are well-known problems of peak-load pricing and so on. General prescriptions cannot be made for these cases. There is a similar ambiguity about the welfare consequences of conditions of sale (including vertical restraints). Where market power is present, we favour a rebuttable presumption against them.

The regulation – by whatever means – of non-price behaviour by a dominant firm poses yet further difficulties. The regulation of quality is an essential complement to the regulation of price wherever quality is at the discretion of the firm being regulated; otherwise price regulation is meaningless. (On quality regulation see Spence, 1975.)

Expenditures on investment and innovation can in principle be regulated, but there are severe practicability problems. Rather than regulate those decisions, it is better to design a system of price or profit regulation that does not greatly distort the input decisions of the dominant firm. After all, the problem with the textbook pure monopolist is that he supplies the wrong output, not that he produces it inefficiently. Nonprice behaviour is of more concern when there is scope for the dominant firm to act in a predatory fashion towards actual or potential rivals, which we have already considered above in connection with the acquisition and maintenance of dominance.

Competition Law in Practice

This section contains a summary and an evaluation of the framework of competition policy in the UK, the EEC, and the USA. The evaluation is based on the principles set out in the previous section. The section concludes with a consideration of two issues – the definition of market shares and the proper administrative structure for competition policy – which are common to all three jurisdictions.

The United Kingdom

The four main elements of competition law in the UK are:

The Fair Trading Act 1973
The Competition Act 1980
The Restrictive Trade Practices Act 1976
The Resale Prices Act 1976

These Acts are not the only pieces of legislation affecting competition matters in the UK. For example, the price controls implemented in the 1970s as part of the government's anti-inflation policy were an important element of competition policy at that time. The current privatization legislation establishes frameworks of competition and regulation for the individual industries concerned. Thus the 1984 Telecommunications Act gives certain powers to the Office of Telecommunications (OFTEL) to monitor conditions of competition in that industry. In addition, there is of course the overarching structure of EEC competition legislation, which we consider separately below. However, in this section we shall concentrate on the Acts listed above, especially the Fair Trading Act and the Competition Act, because they have most bearing on the question of market dominance.

The Fair Trading Act 1973   The Fair Trading Act 1973 consolidated earlier monopolies and mergers legislation and established the Office of Fair Trading (OFT) with responsibilities to monitor competition and consumer affairs.

The post-war development of UK competition legislation prior to this Act can be summarized briefly as follows. The Monopolies (Inquiry and Control) Act 1948 marked the first step by the UK government to take powers concerning competition policy. The Act set up a Monopolies Commission, independent from central government, with responsibilities to investigate and report on cartels and monopolies. The legislation was motivated as much by macroeconomic concerns (e.g. over employment, international competitiveness and price stability) as by microeconomic considerations of efficient resource allocation and effective competition. Accordingly, a loose and wide-ranging concept of the 'public interest' was laid down by the Act as the criterion by which the Monopolies Commission was to assess the effects of cartels or monopolies. A broad definition of the public interest remains with us today.

In its early reports, most notably the general report on collective discrimination, the Commission found collective restrictive practices to be against the public interest, except in special circumstances. Under the Restrictive Trade Practices Act 1956 the investigation and control of cartel agreements was transferred to a Court (see below). Under the Monopolies and Mergers Act 1965 mergers were added to the Commission's responsibilities, and the Commission was renamed the Monopolies and Mergers Commission (MMC).

As regards monopolies, the Fair Trading Act 1973 gives the Secretary of State and the Director-General of Fair Trading (DGFT) powers to refer to the MMC cases where it appears that a 'monopoly situation' exists in relation to the supply or acquisition of goods or services in the UK. A monopoly situation is defined in *legal*, rather than *economic*, terms. It exists where a company (or a group of interconnected companies) accounts for at least 25 per cent of the relevant market. In addition, a 'complex monopoly situation' exists, and may be referred, when two or more companies which together account for at least 25 per cent of the relevant market act so as to restrict competition. Thus the Act embraces oligopolistic dominance to some extent. It is up to the DGFT or minister making the reference to determine which products constitute the relevant market, using the criteria which he believes to be the most appropriate. Note that the definition of a monopoly situation extends to buyers as well as sellers, i.e. to the economist's notion of monopsony.

When a reference is made, the MMC investigates and reports on whether a monopoly situation exists and on whether it operates against the public interest. When the MMC reports that a monopoly situation does have effects which are contrary to the public interest, the Secretary of State may remedy or prevent them by Order. Alternatively he may accept undertakings by the companies in question to refrain from the practices found to be detrimental to the public interest.

Section 84 of the Act lists five criteria to be taken into account in determining the public interest:

1 Maintaining and promoting effective competition between persons supplying goods and services in the United Kingdom;
2 Promoting the interests of consumers, purchasers and other users of goods and services in the United Kingdom in respect of their quality and the variety of goods and services supplied;
3 Promoting, through competition, the reduction of costs and the development and use of new techniques and new products, and facilitating the entry of new competitors into existing markets;
4 Maintaining and promoting the balanced distribution of industry and employment in the United Kingdom; and
5 Maintaining and promoting competitive activity in markets outside the United Kingdom on the part of producers of goods, and of suppliers of goods and services in the United Kingdom.

This broad notion of the public interest, which extends considerably beyond the promotion of effective competition, is also used in merger references and in references under the Competition Act 1980.

As regards mergers, the Fair Trading Act empowers the Secretary of State to refer to the MMC mergers which create or enhance market shares of at least 25 per cent, or which involve assets of more than £30 million. In making a merger reference, the Secretary of State takes advice from the DGFT, who consults the Mergers Panel (a non-statutory interdepartmental committee). When a merger reference is made, the MMC has a limited time (normally no more than six months) in which to investigate and report on whether the merger may be expected to operate against the public interest. Since the question is whether the merger operates *against* the public interest, there is a bias in favour of permitting

mergers, which is aggravated by the very broad notion of the public
interest (see above). In July 1984 the Secretary of State announced the
results of a review of merger policy. He proposed no change to the basic
framework of legislation, but he raised the asset threshold in line with inflation to £30 million. He stated that merger references to the MMC
would be made primarily on competition grounds. References in the past
have not always been primarily on those grounds, and nor have MMC
decisions as to effects upon the public interest.

The Competition Act 1980   One of the principal recommendations in
the 1978 Green Paper on monopolies and mergers policy was that consideration be given to dealing with certain anticompetitive practices of
single firms without full-scale monopoly investigations. This proposal
was made in the light of the fact that the MMC had invariably found
certain anticompetitive practices – including tie-ins, full-line forcing and
some forms of discount – to operate against the public interest. Here
there is a parallel with the development of restrictive practices legislation
in 1956, when consistent MMC findings on cartel arrangements led to the
introduction of new machinery to deal specifically with them.

The Competition Act 1980 implemented the recommendation. Section
2(i) of the Act states that a person engages in an 'anticompetitive
practice' if

> in the course of trade or business that person pursues a course of conduct
> which of itself, or when taken together with a course of conduct pursued by
> persons associated with him, has or is intended to have or is likely to have
> the effect of restricting, distorting or preventing competition in connection
> with the production, supply or acquisition of goods . . . or the supply of
> services in the United Kingdom or any part of it.

Under the Act, the DGFT has power to investigate a company if he
believes that it may be engaged in an anticompetitive practice. After his
investigation, the DGFT reports on whether an anticompetitive practice
exists and on whether reference to the MMC is appropriate. In the latter
event, the OFT may seek undertakings from the company that it will
refrain from the practice. If these are not forthcoming, the DGFT may
refer the matter to the MMC. Then the MMC must determine whether
the course of conduct in question is an anticompetitive practice and
whether it operates against the public interest. The Competition Act
procedure has been used in a number of recent cases concerning, for
example, refusal to supply certain retailers, refusal to supply spare parts,
and predatory pricing. Another major new provision of the Competition

Act empowers the Secretary of State to refer public bodies to the MMC. Several bodies have been referred in this way, including water and electricity authorities and the postal service.

The Restrictive Trade Practices Act 1976 The earlier Restrictive Trade Practices Act 1956 was a result of a series of Monopolies Commission reports on cartels, most importantly that on *Collective Discrimination* (1955), which had identified a set of practices that were found almost always to be against the public interest. The Act embodied the (rebuttable) presumption that such practices should be condemned. The Restrictive Trade Practices Act 1968 provided for the registration of information agreements. The 1976 Act consolidated previous restrictive practices legislation, and was supplemented by a further Act (concerned with financial services) in 1977.

Under the legislation, agreements between two or more companies that involve certain types of restriction must be registered with the DGFT before the restriction comes into effect. Restrictions that are registrable in this way include those on pricing, conditions of supply, and distribution. If a registrable agreement is not registered, it is unenforceable and civil actions to recover damages may be brought by any persons injured by the agreement. It is not clear that the threat of this provides much incentive to register (see Sharpe, 1985). Some types of agreement are exempted from registration, either by statute (as in the case of patents, for example) or, in some circumstances, by order of the Secretary of State. Exclusive dealing agreements are exempted. An important recent example of exemption was the government's announcement in 1983 that it proposed to drop the case against the Stock Exchange under the restrictive practices legislation.

When an agreement is registered with the DGFT, he must bring it to the Restrictive Trade Practices Court (unless he is relieved of this duty by the Secretary of State in the case of innocuous restrictions). The presumption is that the restrictions are against the public interest, and the burden of proof is therefore upon the parties to the agreement to show that they are not. The Act lays down criteria, known as 'gateways', by which restrictions may be justified. If a restriction passes through one or more of these gateways, the Court has finally to decide whether the restriction is not unreasonable in the light of considerations of the public interest.

The Restrictive Trade Practices Acts strike at *explicit* collusion between firms. It was explained above that the Fair Trading Act 1973 embraces market dominance by an oligopoly under the 'complex monopoly' provisions, and therefore tacit collusion is covered to some extent. However, the 1978 Green Paper concluded that existing legislation contained weaknesses in dealing with oligopolies, in particular because under the 1973 Act it must be shown that the oligopolists are acting so as to restrict competition in order for the MMC even to have jurisdiction to investigate. A strengthening of the legislation to include a definition of oligopoly in terms of market structure was recommended but has not been put into effect. This is a theme to which we shall return later.

The Resale Prices Act 1976   This Act, which consolidates earlier legislation including the Resale Prices Act 1964, bans resale price maintenance (RPM), i.e. the practice whereby suppliers enforce minimum prices for the resale of their products. (RPM by a single supplier would not fall under the restrictive practices legislation.) Suppliers can seek exemption from the ban on RPM from the Restrictive Practices Court on public interest grounds. So far only books and pharmaceuticals have obtained exemption. The Resale Prices Act has therefore made vertical restraints involving price almost *per se* illegal. Non-price vertical restraints, however, are treated quite differently: they are condemned only if they are found by the MMC to operate against the public interest in a monopoly investigation under the Fair Trading Act or an anti-competitive practice investigation under the Competition Act. It is odd that non-price restraints should be treated so differently from restraints involving price, since their economic effects can be rather similar.

An evaluation of UK competition law   We now turn to the task of evaluating UK competition law in the light of our earlier discussions on the economic analysis of competition and monopoly and the economics of policy. Our evaluation concerns the general principles that lie behind the policy. The four general principles we enunciated were: that the balance between rules and discretion should have regard to the costs (type I and II errors, and administrative costs) of competition policy; that there should be a presumption in favour of competition, with the onus of proof on those who wish to argue the contrary in a particular instance; that prevention of dominance is better than 'cure'; and that market conduct, however apparently bizarre, should not be the object of policy *unless* effective competition is absent.

It can be argued that competition policy in the UK errs in the direction of being too discretionary. The only non-discretionary elements are the prohibition of resale price maintenance and, in practice, the prohibition of price-fixing agreements between firms. Everything else is the subject of discretionary or administrative procedures. The outcome is *not* that competition policy is more appropriately applied: rather it is that the policy is more sparingly applied, given the costs of a full MMC investigation. A major reason for this discretionary nature of the policy is that the objectives of the policy are very widely defined, in terms of the public interest. This is obviously the case with section 84 of the Fair Trading Act 1973. Of course the aim of public policy should be to further the public interest in some sense, but there is a strong case for giving a public authority such as the MMC an *intermediate* objective such as the promotion and maintenance of effective competition (as in EEC law). The argument is that an antitrust authority should have the specific task of guarding and enhancing the *process* of competition. By contrast, the MMC at present is asked to judge the *consequences* for the public interest (broadly defined) of cases referred to it.

Among the merits of adopting the intermediate objective of promoting effective competition are that the MMC would have a better defined criterion on which to operate, its deliberations would be simplified, and greater predictability of its decisions would result. Moreover, competition criteria would be the basis for MMC deliberations, whereas at present the MMC spends much time deliberating matters that have little to do with competition (see Kay and Silberston, 1984). There is the drawback that the promotion of effective competition is sometimes in conflict with other factors – for example the desirability of improving productive efficiency by the achievement of scale economies. One way to accommodate this point would be to adopt a rebuttable presumption in favour of effective competition, with the onus of proof on those seeking to establish that the benefits of other factors outweigh those of competition. Such a solution is already part of restrictive practices legislation. It would make competition considerations clearly the most important, whereas at present it is not clear how the various components of the 'public interest' are to be weighed by the MMC.

Our third principle is that prevention is better than cure in policy towards dominance. This has not been a major priority for competition policy in the UK. The obvious example is policy towards mergers. We note that the present bias of policy is in favour of permitting mergers. We believe that is broadly acceptable in respect of vertical and conglomerate mergers, but wrong in respect of horizontal mergers. The 1978 Green Paper *A Review of Monopolies and Mergers Policy* recommended that the current bias in favour of permitting mergers should go. The Liesner Committee, which produced the Green Paper, reviewed the evidence relating to the importance of merger in accounting for increasing concentration in UK industry, and that relating to the effect of merger on the economic performance of the firms involved, and concluded that there were no good reasons for a permissive policy. Our view is that the presumption should be reversed if there is reason to believe that the merger is detrimental to effective competition. Mergers should then be permitted only if the *parties* can demonstrate substantial social gains in terms of economic efficiency, sufficient to offset any losses from increased market power.

The fourth principle is that policy should concern itself with market conduct only if there are reasons to believe that effective competition is absent. The broad criterion of the public interest used in cases of monopolies, mergers, and alleged anticompetitive practices is such that this principle is not always followed. For example, monopoly and merger references may be made if market shares exceed given percentages. These percentages and the markets themselves need not be defined in economic terms: the definition of monopoly is in legal terms. Once a reference has been made, the job of the MMC is to judge its effects in terms of the public interest – a notion that includes many things other than effects on competition. Thus the MMC might decide that a practice was against the public interest even though effective competition existed in the market in question. The problem is compounded by the broad definition of anticompetitive practice in the 1980 Competition Act.

Some confusion has arisen here concerning the respective roles of the OFT and the MMC in judging public interest implications (see the discussion of the Raleigh case in Kay and Sharpe, 1982). The broad definition of anticompetitive practice has sometimes been taken by the OFT to include any course of conduct that affects competition in the sense that rivals may lose market share or leave the market, whether or not the conduct is a distortion of the competitive process. Interpreting the definition so broadly is undesirable in two respects. First, there is a temptation for the OFT to make judgements, albeit implicitly, about the public interest, which is really the job of the MMC. Secondly, there is a tendency for the investigation of the existence of market power to be left to the MMC, whereas it should be done by the OFT under the Competition Act procedure. Thus the division of labour between OFT and MMC has on occasions been obscured. Some clarification of the position was made in the MMC report on Sheffield newspapers, where the MMC distinguished between conduct that restricts, distorts, or prevents competition, and conduct that otherwise affects competition. The distinction is between effects on the process of competition as opposed to effects on competitors. To give substance to the distinction it is important that the OFT investigates the existence and effect of the market power of the company involved. It is inadequate to jump from the fulfilment of a broad definition of anticompetitive practices to an assessment of the effects upon the public interest. An assessment of the existence and possible abuse of market dominance should be a necessary part of the investigation.

Two other issues arising from our consideration of UK competition policy are not dealt with here, because we shall see that these are general issues that arise in the US and the EEC as well. One is the vexed issue of the definition of dominance in terms of market share. The other is the legal and administrative framework for competition policy. On this we merely note, for the moment, the reliance of UK monopolies and mergers policy (as opposed to restrictive practices policy) on administrative rather than judicial procedures, in contrast to the US.

The European Economic Community

EEC competition policy is one of the means used to pursue the overall objective of a unified common market between member states. Article 3(f) of the Treaty of Rome calls for 'the institution of a system ensuring that competition is not distorted'. Competition policy is thus complementary to policies that abolish institutional obstacles to trade between member states such as tariffs and quotas. Its purpose is to ensure that private parties do not frustrate market integration by way of anticompetitive practices. Competition is seen as being essential to securing the aims of the Treaty and the stimulation of economic activity. In contrast to the broad 'public interest' approach in the UK, under EEC policy overriding importance is attached to promoting and maintaining effective competition.

The main provisions of EEC competition law are articles 85 and 86 of the Treaty of Rome. Article 85 prohibits and declares void agreements and concerted practices which have the object or effect of preventing, restricting, or distorting competition within the EEC and which affect trade between member states. Horizontal, vertical, price, and non-price restrictions all fall under the provisions of article 85. Restrictive agreements and practices must be notified to the Commission, but exemption from prohibition may be sought under article 85(3) on the grounds that they contribute 'to improving the production or distribution of goods or to promoting technical or economic progress'. However, exemption may not be granted if the restrictions are not necessary to the attainment of those objectives, or if they involve the risk of eliminating competition.

Article 86 of the Treaty is concerned with market dominance. It condemns

> any abuse by one or more undertakings of a dominant position within the Common Market or a substantial part of it . . . in so far as it may affect trade between Member States. Such abuse may, in particular, consist in:
>
> (a) directly or indirectly imposing unfair purchasing or selling prices or other unfair trading conditions;
> (b) limiting production, markets or technical development to the prejudice of consumers;
> (c) applying dissimilar conditions to equivalent transactions with other trading parties, thereby placing them at a competitive disadvantage;
> (d) making the conclusion of contracts subject to acceptance by the other parties of supplementary obligations which, by their nature or according to commercial usage, have no connection with the subject of such contracts.

The European Commission has powers under Council regulation 17 of 1962 to investigate suspected breaches of articles 85 and 86, to require the termination of practices that are found to infringe them, and to impose fines of up to 10 per cent of the annual worldwide turnover of the guilty parties. The Commission may begin an investigation on its own initiative or following complaints received from affected parties. It has extensive investigatory powers. The Commission must allow representations from interested parties before making a final decision. In some circumstances the Commission also has powers to impose interim measures before reaching a final decision. Competition matters are the province of Directorate-General IV (DG IV) within the Commission.

The European Court of Justice has wide-ranging powers of judicial review over Commission decisions, and appeal has been made to the Court against many Commission decisions under articles 85 and 86. By this means the Court has shaped EEC competition policy to a considerable extent. In the case of *Hoffman–La Roche* the Court defined a dominant position as a position of economic strength enjoyed by an undertaking which enables it to prevent effective competition being maintained on the relevant market by affording it the power to behave to an appreciable extent independently of its competitors, its customers and ultimately of the consumers.

Note that dominance exists in relation to a 'relevant product market', and market definition therefore becomes a central part of any case. Indeed, the enquiry into dominance becomes divided into two parts – *first* the definition of the relevant product market, and *then* the investigation of dominance within that 'market'. Once dominance has been established, there is then the question of whether abuse has occurred.

An evaluation of EEC competition law The importance of effective competition is central to EEC competition policy, and is an instrument used to promote the wider objective of a unified common market. As regards dominance, article 86 appears to be concerned to check the exercise of dominance, rather than its acquisition or maintenance. EEC law has weaknesses in relation to the acquisition of market power. No explicit provisions exist at present for the scrutiny of mergers, and by its nature EEC law can do little to prevent the grant of domestic market power by national governments.

However, the recent AKZO case on predatory pricing is an important example of how EEC law can strike at attempts to acquire and maintain dominance. AKZO was found to have infringed article 86 by abusing a dominant position in the EEC organic peroxides market. AKZO threatened a small rival so as to deter it from entering a new market. When the threat was ignored, AKZO implemented a strategy of selective below-cost pricing to exclude the rival from the market. AKZO was fined heavily and prohibited from using the predatory practices in future.

Two controversial issues in article 86 cases have been the principles of market definition (and its role in the inference of market dominance), and the Commission's tendency in some cases to condemn particular forms of conduct as abusive without full prior investigation of dominance. The first of these issues arises not only in EEC antitrust, and we consider it more generally at the end of this section. We turn now to the second question – the relationship between dominance and abuse in article 86 cases.

In their paper on the economics of article 86, Fairburn et al. (1984) argue that 'the Court has generally sought to identify abuse and, having done so, has generally found it possible to define a market such that the abuse is an abuse of a dominant position within the market.' The

Michelin case perhaps exemplifies these points. The Commission, who were upheld by the Court, condemned Michelin's policy of giving annual bonuses to dealers who had performed well relative to sales targets. The policy was condemned as a loyalty rebate designed to tie dealers to Michelin. Moreover, the practices found to be abusive were central to the argument that Michelin had market power. Hay (1985b) criticizes the decision on the grounds that in the absence of evidence of predatory pricing, the basic objection seems to be that Michelin made its dealers an offer too attractive to refuse, which is close to then saying that it is anticompetitive for Michelin successfully to raise its market share. On the other hand, it can happen that loyalty rebates diminish competition by causing there to be switching costs, but analysis of the particular facts is required. In addition, the Court upheld the Commission's view that Michelin's market share of 65 per cent justified the conclusion of dominance. The market was defined as the market for heavy tyres in the Netherlands, although it can perhaps be contended that there is significant competition – actual and potential – from suppliers of other types of tyre, and from other parts of the EEC, especially in view of the overcapacity in the industry.

In principle there is no circularity in inferring dominance from conduct, and for the conduct to be regarded as an abuse. Suppose, for example, that a supplier persistently charged very different prices for the same product in two distinct markets, and that he could provide no justification for his discriminatory practice. This conduct is evidence of dominance, and, given a finding of dominance, could well be judged to be an abuse. The reason why such conduct points to dominance is that it could be practised persistently only by a dominant firm: it can be demonstrated that effective competition would see to the erosion of unjustified price differences. However, *pace* the Commission, it is not obvious that (say) discounts to dealers could be practised *only* by a dominant firm. In the absence of independent argument to that end, there is in effect outright condemnation of the practice, irrespective of the existence of dominance.

At this point one can go in either of two directions. The first is indeed to condemn certain types of conduct whether or not they are accompanied by dominance (as with RPM in the UK, for example). The second is to retain the principle that the process of effective competition is by and large the best way to promote economic well-being, and to insist that dominance be established before abuse can be found. The latter view is quite consistent with the firm's conduct providing evidence of dominance as long as there is independent reason to think that the conduct could be practised only by a dominant firm. Although we are not subscribers to the view that competition is always for the very best, we do believe that in an imperfect world the only sensible basis for policy is the general (though rebuttable) presumption that without dominance there cannot be abuse. Where effective competition prevails, market forces are generally as likely as antitrust authorities to produce good results.

The United States of America

The founding statutes of American competition law are the Sherman Act of 1890, the Clayton Act of 1914 and the Federal Trade Commission Act of 1914. This early legislation was inspired as much by the desire to protect political liberties as by the view that competition is the mainspring of economic progress. The Acts embody a vigorous procompetitive spirit in legal form, and are far removed from the *ad hoc* approach that characterizes competition policy in the UK.

The Sherman Act prohibits two broad classes of anticompetitive behaviour. Section 1 prohibits contracts, combinations and conspiracies in restraint of trade. Section 2 outlaws monopolization, attempts to monopolize and conspiracies to monopolize. Being federal law, the Act applies to trade between states and with foreign nations. There are criminal penalties, including fines and imprisonment, for violations. Actions could be brought either by public authority, in the name of the Attorney-General, or by private parties, who could sue under the Act for three times the damages inflicted upon them by violators of the law. In amended form these provisions remain today.

The Clayton Act of 1914 supplemented the Sherman Act by specifying certain practices as anticompetitive. Section 2, which was amended by the Robinson-Patman Act in 1936, outlawed price discrimination with an adverse effect on competition. Section 3 prohibited certain vertical restraints (such as tie-ins) that are detrimental to competition. Section 7 dealt with anticompetitive mergers, and was strengthened in 1950 by the Celler-Kefauver amendment.

The Federal Trade Commission Act of 1914 set up an agency, the FTC, with investigatory and quasi-judicial powers over competition matters. The Act also prohibited 'unfair methods of competition' in loose terms. The FTC shares the task of enforcing the antitrust laws with the Antitrust Division of the Justice Department. The division of labour between them is not always totally clear. In addition, there is of course an important role for private litigants who can bring treble damages cases (see later) under the Sherman Act.

There are important exemptions from antitrust law, especially concerning labour, agriculture, and regulated industries. The Webb-Pomerene Act of 1918 exempts agreements solely concerned with exporting which have no effect on domestic competition.

In the remainder of this section we consider some landmark cases in the evolution of American antitrust law, and we briefly describe the guidelines on mergers and on vertical restraints recently issued by the Department of Justice.

The evolution of US antitrust case law   Having described the basic structure of US antitrust law, we now consider how some of the major cases concerned with market dominance gave further shape to the law.

Perhaps the most important cases under section 2 of the Sherman Act in the early years of the century were Standard Oil in 1911 and US Steel in 1915. In the Standard Oil case the Supreme Court upheld the district court's finding of guilt, and ordered the dissolution of Standard Oil of New Jersey into 33 regional companies. The Supreme Court held that monopolization consists of two things: the acquisition of monopoly position, and the intent to acquire that position and to exclude rivals. The Court ruled that Standard Oil's intent could be inferred from its predatory conduct. In the same year the Court made a similar ruling against American Tobacco, and again imposed the remedy of structural break-up. In the US Steel case a four-to-three majority of the Supreme Court ruled in favour of the company, saying that 'the law does not make mere size an offense or the existence of unexerted power an offense. It requires . . . overt acts.' The case established the rule that the mere possession of monopoly power was not an offence.

The post-war cases of Alcoa and United Shoe Machinery represented major developments in antitrust law. Whereas Standard Oil had acquired and maintained its market dominance by illegal means, Alcoa and United Shoe owed their market power to lawful means that were described as 'honestly industrial' although 'not economically inevitable'. Because their respective dominant positions were due to choice, the courts nevertheless found the companies guilty of monopolization under section 2 of the Sherman Act. Thus illegal acts were no longer necessary for there to be monopolization.

The Alcoa case in 1945 resulted from an appeal by the Justice Department against an earlier district court finding in Alcoa's favour. The

Supreme Court being inquorate, the case was heard by a panel of circuit court judges, with Judge Learned Hand presiding. Market definition and the analysis of market shares were central to the finding of dominance. The court favoured the narrowest of the three principal definitions, and Alcoa's resulting market share of 90 per cent was judged to be enough to constitute monopoly. However, Judge Hand acknowledged that a high market share did not necessarily imply monopolization. Rather, it could be the result of 'superior skill, foresight, and industry', which competition of course aims to promote.

As to Alcoa's intent to monopolize, Judge Hand declared that

Nothing compelled [Alcoa] to keep doubling and redoubling its capacity before others entered the field. It insists that it never excluded competitors; but we can think of no more effective exclusion than progressively to embrace each new opportunity as it opened and to face every newcomer with new capacity already geared into a great organization, having the advantage of experience, trade connections and the elite of personnel.

The court's statement is a most eloquent description of what would now be called strategic entry deterrence by means of excess capacity (see Schmalensee's paper in this volume). Judge Hand also stated that 'drastic expenditures on research and development with knowledge or intent to pre-empt and dominate an industry' could be a violation of section 2 of the Sherman Act. Economists have recently studied pre-emptive patenting and the persistence of monopoly in a similar spirit (see Gilbert and Newbery, 1982).

The United Shoe decision was less radical than that in the Alcoa case, but was in similar vein. United Shoe had enjoyed a high and stable share of a static market for many years, and only one small firm had successfully entered the industry in recent years. The Supreme Court found United Shoe guilty of monopolization, even though its practices were not condemned as illegal in themselves. Among the practices that were held to deter entry were United Shoe's refusal to sell machines; contract terms that encouraged customers to lease its full line of machines; and a pricing structure that yielded high profits on the parts of United's business protected by patents. Other major cases that followed the Alcoa precedent involved cinema chains and the A & P Company, a food retailing concern.

Market definition was again at the centre of the Cellophane case in 1956. A majority of the Supreme Court did not find du Pont guilty of monopolizing the Cellophane industry. By virtue of patents du Pont controlled the production of Cellophane, but the question was the substitutability between Cellophane and other types of wrapping. Du Pont's share of the market for flexible packaging materials in general was less than one-fifth. The Court found that other types of packaging were interchangeable and competitive, and did not find monopolization. Thus arguments about definitions largely determined the outcome (despite the Court's uncertainties over the application of market definition tests).

The 1970s saw a number of major antitrust cases, most notably those involving AT & T and IBM. Both mammoth cases ended in January 1982. Under a consent decree, AT & T was divested of its local operating companies and retained its long-distance division and manufacturing subsidiary. The company was allowed to compete in markets – such as data processing – in which it had not previously been allowed to compete. The AT & T decision reflects the growing disillusionment in the United States with traditional public utility regulation (for an account of the regulated telecommunications industry in particular see Brock, 1981). The decision attempted to give freer rein to the forces of competition so as to lessen the 'burden' of regulation.

The IBM case was initiated on the last day of President Johnson's administration in 1969. As well as the Department of Justice case against IBM, the company faced numerous treble damages actions throughout the 1970s, and in 1980 received a Statement of Objections from the European Commission under article 86 of the Treaty of Rome. The private actions under section 2 of the Sherman Act were all eventually settled, or decided in IBM's favour. The EEC case was settled in August 1984. The settlement is concerned with, among other things, the provision by IBM of 'interface information' to its competitors following the announcement by IBM of new products.

In the IBM case market definition was once again to the fore. The Department of Justice defined the market as being for 'general-purpose' electronic digital computer systems. The definition excluded suppliers of components of systems and also suppliers of 'special-purpose' systems (which included, for example, minicomputers). When Telex won in the district court in 1973 three additional submarkets were defined – those for IBM-plug-compatible disk drives, tape drives, and memory devices. IBM, on the other hand, argued for a broader definition, to include, for example, parts of systems and systems not classified as general purpose. Market share depended critically upon which definition was adopted (and also upon the method of measuring the share empirically).

The IBM case raises fascinating questions concerning dominance in industries in which there is a high rate of technological advance. IBM's pre-eminence in the industry in the 1960s was due to its skill, foresight, and industry in perceiving and meeting the potential demand for data processing services. The IBM System/360, announced in 1964, was a revolutionary range of systems. It offered extensive intrarange compatibility for the first time, giving users much greater flexibility, and its transistor-based technology provided a remarkable improvement in price performance. The central question in the litigation was whether IBM's continued pre-eminence in the 1970s was due to continued skill, foresight, and industry or to anticompetitive abuse of the position previously gained. The Department of Justice questioned IBM's strategies towards new entry, in particular some of its pricing practices (including bundling and leasing). Differing accounts of IBM's position in the industry are given by Brock (1975) and Fisher et al. (1983).

The case went to trial in 1975, six years after proceedings began. In June 1981 William Baxter, the Assistant Attorney-General in charge of the Antitrust Division in the Reagan administration, began a review of the case. He concluded that 'the case is without merit and should be dismissed', and the stipulation of dismissal was issued on 8 January 1982, nearly thirteen years after the initiation of the case. Whatever may be one's view of the merits of the case, the episode is hardly satisfactory. In terms of the enormous amounts of time and resources devoted to it, the IBM litigation breaks all records. Naturally, the litigation has provoked considerable debate about the conduct of antitrust policy. Some argued that the antitrust laws and procedures were obsolete. Others (see e.g. Fisher et al., 1983) argued that the antitrust laws, and judicial interpretations of them, are not outmoded, and that the fiasco of the IBM case was in part due to the unsound economic analysis of the government's economists. Yet others regarded the case against IBM as sound, and saw its dismissal as a reflection of a more tolerant approach to big business under the Reagan administration.

Be that as it may, the influence of economic thinking upon US antitrust policy has grown considerably, as is documented by George Hay's paper in this volume. Moreover, recent antitrust cases have greatly influenced the development of the economic theory. We have already suggested that cases such as IBM raised important questions about dominance in technologically progressive industries – about conversion costs, standards, and compatibility (see Katz and Shapiro, 1985).

A number of recent antitrust cases have stimulated developments in economic theory. The FTC case against producers of ready-to-eat (RTE) breakfast cereals is an example. The charge was one of collective monopolization by four companies who accounted for 90 per cent of the market for RTE breakfast cereals. The business was characterized by lack of entry, apparent parallelism of conduct, high profits, very high advertising, and the proliferation of product brands. Schmalensee (1978) showed how the proliferation of product brands can serve as a device that deters entry at the same time as permitting high profit margins.

Similarly, recent economic theories of pre-emptive patenting have stemmed from antitrust cases, for example those involving Xerox. In 1975 an FTC case against Xerox was settled when Xerox agreed to license its range of plain-paper copier patents at reasonable rates of royalty. The company was also involved in private actions in the United States, and in an MMC enquiry in the UK, where Rank Xerox's monopoly position was regarded as a just reward for its innovative efforts and not against the public interest. As in the IBM case, the Xerox litigation was about dominance in an innovative industry.

Justice Department Guidelines   The recent Justice Department Guidelines on mergers and vertical restraints provide a further illustration of the increasing importance of economics in the formulation of American antitrust policy (see Hay's paper in this volume for further discussion of this point; and see Hay, 1985a). In particular they represent a move away from the 'structure-conduct-performance' approach, in which market structure is seen as the prime determinant of industry conduct and performance, and they accord more importance to potential competition than was previously the case.

US Department of Justice Guidelines do not have binding force. They are simply an indication of when the Justice Department will and will not bring cases, and as such they contribute towards the predictability of antitrust enforcement. The courts, the FTC and private parties are not bound by the Guidelines, but they are undoubtedly influenced by them to some extent.

The 1968 Merger Guidelines laid down structural criteria – based on market shares – for challenging mergers. Conditions of entry played little role. The market share tests had the merit of being relatively simple to apply. For example, in an industry where the four-firm concentration ratio exceeded 75 per cent, the Justice Department would challenge a merger between a firm with a market share greater than 15 per cent and one with a share of more than 1 per cent.

The Merger Guidelines were revised in 1982. The new Guidelines retain the 'numerical', market shares approach, but incorporate the role of potential competition explicitly within it. The relevant market shares are those in the *hypothetical* situation that would result if prices in the industry were raised 5 per cent above their status quo level for a sustained period. Market shares in this hypothetical situation might be quite different from market shares in the status quo, and therefore the 1982 Guidelines may differ markedly in effect from those of 1968. The Herfindahl Index (see Hay and Morris, 1979, pp. 104–7) is used to measure concentration, and changes therein due to merger, in the hypothetical situation arising from the 5 per cent price increase.

The hypothetical price increases would encourage firms supplying other products and other geographic areas to supply the industry in question. Thus the Guidelines take account of 'supply substitutability'. Completely new entry is not incorporated into the calculation, but if entry is evidently easy the merger is likely to be unchallenged anyway. The 1982 Guidelines did not clarify exactly how potential foreign competitors were to be incorporated into the analysis. The conservative view was adopted that overseas suppliers face constraints that limit their ability to expand in the domestic market. Thus overseas and domestic suppliers were initially treated differently under the Guidelines. However, in 1984 the Guidelines were amended so that all suppliers – foreign and domestic – are to be treated alike in the reckoning of potential competition. The argument is that where a foreign supplier has significant domestic sales it has evidently overcome whatever barriers there may be, and so virtually all its global capacity may be incorporated into the market share calculation. In theory the 1984 amendment to the Guidelines therefore means that foreign firms could be accorded very large 'shares' in the hypothetical situation envisaged, and that correspondingly small shares would be ascribed to the parties to the merger. Under the new Guidelines, the Department of Justice will admit considerations of efficiency to be set against the detriment to competition in assessing a merger.

Several criticisms can be made of the Guidelines. The first (see Hay, 1985a, p. 70) is that they do not provide the predictability that was their original aim. The hypothetical market shares are difficult and controversial to calculate, and efficiency may be claimed as a defence of a merger even when the share criteria are breached. Secondly, if a merger resulted in a price increase, it is not clear that other firms would respond in the way that they would respond to a *sustained* price increase of the sort hypothesized in the Guidelines. That is because the profitability of supplying the market depends on the price that would result after supply substitution. The (plausible) prospect of price reduction in the event of supply substitution means that the hypothesized sustained increase in price might not provide an appropriate test. Thirdly, the Guidelines are subject to many of the criticisms concerning market definition made earlier. They do however take explicit account of some forms of entry, albeit in a controversial manner.

The Department of Justice Vertical Restraint Guidelines adopt a similar approach (see Hay, 1985a). Non-price restraints are perfectly legal in industries where concentration (measured hypothetically as above) is low, or where a low proportion of the industry practises the restraint. Tie-ins, for example, are held to be of no concern unless the firm in question has more than 30 per cent of the market. As Hay observes, the recently permissive attitude in the United States towards vertical restraints is to be contrasted with practice in the UK and the EEC.

The future course of US antitrust policy   In the first term of the Reagan presidency, American antitrust policy was rationalized. Fewer resources were devoted to antitrust enforcement and, as George Hay documents in this volume, policy was subjected more to economic analysis. The most recent developments are moves to restrict the scope of the antitrust laws. A number of bills sent to Congress early in 1986 propose relaxation of antitrust policy with a view to promoting the international competitiveness of American companies. For example, enhanced international competitiveness is allowed as a merger defence. It is also proposed that the President be empowered to give antitrust exemptions for up to five years to companies threatened by overseas competition, provided that they do not benefit from certain trade remedies.

These proposals continue earlier trends – for example the 1984 Merger Guidelines. They reflect a much less interventionist approach in US antitrust policy, and they are a way of satisfying pressures from business interests without building too many barriers to trade. Protectionism is bad, and free trade is an important complement to antitrust policy. But there are grave dangers in a weakening of domestic antitrust policy. It remains to be seen what Congress makes of the proposals before it.

Evaluation of US competition policy   It will be apparent from the preceding pages that in the past US antitrust policy has been closer to our notion of what competition policy should be than that of the UK or the EEC. The statutes and the case law have generally embodied a strong presumption in favour of the competitive process. Those who wish to argue the contrary in a particular case are cast very much in the role of defendants who are accused of not observing the rules of the competitive game. There is an emphasis on prevention of dominance as well as measures to deal with the exercise of dominance. The Guidelines on vertical restraints have recently embodied the principle that competition policy should not concern itself with market conduct in the absence of dominance.

The US competition authorities have become more aware in recent years of the dangers of regulatory capture. There is therefore less willingness to renew or make grants of monopoly. Regulated sectors have been opened up to competition, and attention has been paid to the possibility of breaking up regulated monopolies. The legal framework has long been inimical to collusive practices and mergers, though the problems of tacit collusion have exercised US antitrust authorities just as much as their European counterparts. The distinction between dominance acquired by skill, foresight, and industry, and that gained by predation, has also proved a stumbling block in the application of policy. In respect of the maintenance of dominance, the Merger Guidelines make it clear that the question of potential competition is to be taken into account. The role of entry in preventing a dominant firm from exploiting its position is thereby given prominence, even though this is not an emphasis which is present in the legislation. Finally, in respect of the exercise of dominance, the policy has not shrunk from ordering the dissolution of dominant firms, and in principle at least takes a definite line on market conduct by dominant firms, which is designed to enhance their dominance.

Our contention is, therefore, that UK and EEC competition policies have much to learn from the US example. US policy has, in recent years at least, been much more willing to incorporate insights from economic analysis. These have fitted in well with the long-term emphasis of US legislation on the promotion of competition, in particular by the prevention of dominance. The determination to prevent the acquisition of dominance has been present only weakly in UK and EEC competition policy. Increasing emphasis has been placed on the question of entry and potential entry, in response to the publicity accorded to contestability theory. Despite our reservations about this theory we agree that the consideration of entry should be a key issue in policy. What is more disturbing about US antitrust policy is its possible future course in the face of protectionist pressures.

General Policy Issues

Next we consider two key issues for competition policy in all three jurisdictions – the definition of market shares as part of the process of determining dominance, and the proper administrative structure for competition policy, including the relative merits of judicial and administrative procedures.

Market definition and market shares   Competition authorities attach great importance to market share figures in antitrust proceedings involving market dominance. Perhaps the most famous statement of all about market shares is in Judge Learned Hand's opinion in the Alcoa case in 1945 when he declared that a share of more than 90 per cent 'is enough to constitute a monopoly; it is doubtful whether 60 or 64 per cent would be enough; and certainly 33 per cent is not.' Similarly, the European Court of Justice in the Hoffman–La Roche case shared the view of the European Commission that market shares between 63 and 100 per cent were presumptive of dominance, but the Court did not agree that Roche's share of the market for vitamin B3, which was between 29 and 51 per cent, indicated dominance. In the United Brands case, a market share of 40–5 per cent was found by the European Court to be significant (especially in view of the smallness of rivals' shares), but not conclusive of dominance. Under the Fair Trading Act in the UK, a market share of 25 per cent is necessary and sufficient for the DGFT to have the power to refer a case to the MMC, and the MMC has used market share data in arriving at decisions regarding the public interest.

Judgements relating market shares to market power make market definition of the essence. Thus Merkin and Williams (1985, p. 135) in their recent text on competition law write: 'Generally, the more narrowly the market is defined, the easier it becomes to conclude that a firm has a dominant position. . . . However, the possibility of dominance becomes increasingly remote as the market is widened.' This remark, which concerns the interpretation of the law, does not accord with an economist's way of thinking. For an economist, the issue is the degree of power of the firm persistently to behave in a manner independent of its rivals in making its business decisions. The ready availability of products substitutable with those of the firm is one factor that might constrain its market power, and hence it is important to assess the degree to which they are available. If undertaken with this in mind, market definition can be a valuable part of the overall investigation of dominance (although the term is perhaps rather misleading). However, there is a danger that so much importance is attached to the semantics of market definition that the real question of dominance is prejudged, or at any rate greatly influenced, by how the world is described. The quotation above illustrates this danger rather clearly.

In one sense it ought not to matter how the market is defined. A narrow definition produces a high share, but excludes forces acting upon the firm from outside the market. Provided that proper account is taken of the latter forces, no harm is done, although the share of the narrow market may be a pretty meaningless percentage. A broad definition may embrace the forces that were external to the narrow market, but may also include products whose presence impinges little upon the firm being investigated. Again, allowance can be made for this. Whatever definition is adopted, the ultimate answer should in principle be the same. However, the importance attached to market definition in antitrust cases suggests that this is unfortunately far from being so. The notion of *the* relevant product market is therefore a dangerous one.

Moreover, the assessment of the degree of substitutability between products cannot properly be separated from other aspects of the dominance investigation. The conventional measure of the degree of demand substitutability between two products is their cross-elasticity of demand. The cross-elasticity of demand for product X with respect to the price of product Y is defined as the proportional change in the demand for X divided by the associated proportional change in the price of Y. It is worth noting that the cross-elasticity of X with respect to the price of Y may differ substantially from the cross-elasticity of Y with respect to the price of X. This makes it awkward to define markets in terms of cross-elasticity, for it could happen that X is in the same market as Y but not vice versa. A measure of substitutability that avoids this asymmetry problem is the marginal rate of substitution, which measures how the ratio of X to Y varies with their relative price.

There is a second, and far more important, reason why the cross-elasticity of demand may be an unsuitable measure of substitutability (assuming, heroically, that it can be observed). It is that the elasticity is a function of the prices of the products, including that of the firm being investigated. A firm with market power might well choose a price at which the cross-elasticity of demand for its product is quite high. Indeed, we know that all profit-maximizing firms (including monopolists) operate where the *own*-price elasticity of demand for their products is elastic. Thus there is a danger in using observed cross-elasticities as a guide to appropriate market definition in dominance investigations.

Several EEC antitrust cases have raised a particular question concerning market definition, namely the importance of a *subset* of consumers who have no real alternative to the products of the firm under investigation. For example, in the United Brands case, one of the main grounds on which bananas were distinguished from other fruit was the fact that some consumers – the old, the young, and the infirm – were dependent upon them. A related issue is 'lock-in', which occurs when consumers face switching costs if they change their supplier (von Weizsäcker, 1984). For example, in the Hugin case the Commission's definition of the relevant product market, which the Court upheld, was for spare parts for Hugin cash registers. Again, the argument for the manufacturer-specific definition was that users of Hugin cash registers had no alternative but to go to Hugin for their spare parts.

In these various cases, there arises the general question of how much weight should be given to the fact (if it be a fact) that a *subset* of consumers has little real choice open to it. If such a group is being exploited, in the sense that it faces unfavourable discriminatory terms of supply, then it forms a submarket in which dominance is evident. The discriminatory behaviour of the supplier is itself evidence of dominance (and may also constitute abuse: see below). However, if all consumers are treated alike, it is hard to see why any *extra* weight should be accorded to those with inelastic demands. There are plenty of reasons why a firm would not discriminate against such a group of consumers, even if it could do so, including the preservation of its reputation (or the fear of falling foul of the antitrust authorities!). In the absence of discrimination, the firm's behaviour depends on the sum of the demands of the various consumers, and the aggregate demand for its product is therefore what matters. Of course the consumers with inelastic demand form part of the aggregate, but there is no reason why they should carry more weight than other consumers in the overall reckoning.

So far we have looked at substitutability on the demand side. We conclude this section by discussing supply substitutability as a principle of market definition. Product X is said to be supply substitutable with product Y if the resources currently employed in the supply of X could readily be switched to product Y. In the case of Continental Can the European Court of Justice recognized the importance of supply substitutability in defining the relevant product market. The Court faulted the Commission's definition of separate markets for meat cans and fish cans on the grounds that suppliers of one type of can could readily switch resources to supply the other type.

Any analysis of market power must assess the possible competitive force described as supply substitutability just as it must assess potential competition to the allegedly dominant firm in general. However, the notion of supply substitutability as a principle of market definition is in some ways an awkward one. If suppliers of X switched the use of their resources so as to supply Y, we would have a type of entry into the activity of supplying Y. It is probably more illuminating to consider this sort of potential competition along with other potential competition, rather than to accord it different status by including it in the relevant product market in a somewhat roundabout fashion. This is not to deny that some forms of potential competition are likely to operate more swiftly than others; it is simply to distinguish between actual and potential competition, and to avoid confusing mixtures of the two.

Although in principle there is much to be said for distinguishing between actual and potential competition – and accordingly considering supply substitutability as part of the latter – there is perhaps a practical reason for maintaining it as a principle of market definition. It is that if market share figures are given too much weight in dominance investigations, and if correspondingly little weight is attached to potential competition from outside the market, then the use of supply substitutability in market definition corrects the balance to the extent that it causes some aspects of potential competition to be taken more fully into account, albeit by the back door of market definition.

The administration of competition policy   We conclude this section on policy in practice by comparing the administration of antitrust policy in the UK, the EEC, and the USA. Procedures differ according to whether they are primarily judicial or administrative, and according to the scope allowed to private parties in the enforcement of competition policy.

UK competition policy is monopolized by public authorities: there is no scope for private actions. Policy is an odd combination of the judicial and the administrative (see Sharpe, 1985). Restrictive practices, for example, are in the domain of a court, and the emphasis is on legal form rather than economic effects. On the other hand, monopolies, mergers,

and anticompetitive practices are handled by a combination of government ministers, the Office of Fair Trading, and the Monopolies and
Mergers Commission. These political and administrative bodies focus
more on economic effects than on legal form. The division of labour between them is not always clear, as was shown by some recent merger
cases and the treatment of restrictive practices in the Stock Exchange.
The scale of ministerial intervention in the UK is not surprising given the
statutory framework, but its effect is to confuse the workings of the competition authorities, because considerations having little to do with competition can come to loom large. Private parties play little role apart
from providing evidence to the MMC, and lobbying.

The EEC competition policy is administered by the European Commission (DG IV in particular) subject to judicial review by the European
Court of Justice. Actions under articles 85 and 86 may also be brought
by private parties in the courts of the member states. In the EEC there is
vertical division of labour between the Commission and the Court, with
the Court at the higher level, whereas in the UK the division of labour is
horizontal, with Court and Commission dealing with different subject
matters. In principle the European Court addresses itself only to matters
of law, while the Commission investigates the facts. However, the Court
has addressed questions of economic analysis such as market definition
and supply substitutability. In addition, there is judicial review in the
sense that private parties could bring proceedings against the Commission before the Court if the Commission were not complying with the
principles of due process and good administration.

American antitrust policy is the most judicial in character. Although
the Justice Department and the Federal Trade Commission have powers
of antitrust enforcement, the courts play the major role. The public
authorities have initiated most of the landmark antitrust cases, for
example AT & T and IBM in recent years, but private actions account for
a large proportion of American antitrust activity. A successful plaintiff
may be awarded three times the damages inflicted upon him by the antitrust violations of the defendant company. This possibility of treble
damages greatly encourages the bringing of private antitrust suits,
especially when lawyers' fees are made contingent on the outcome of the
case. Indeed, the plaintiff may have virtually nothing to lose by bringing
the action. It can be argued that these arrangements offer too much
encouragement to 'vexatious litigation' – i.e. actions brought with a view
to inducing even innocent defendants to settle with plaintiffs simply to
avoid legal action.

The possibility of vexatious litigation is one argument against permitting private actions under UK competition law. (Private actions in the UK can of course be brought under EEC law.) However, the danger of such litigation is lessened if the multiple of damages is not so great, and if contingency fees are not allowed. Another argument against private actions in the UK is that it would be beyond the reasonable capacity of the courts to deal with them. The same argument applies against any proposals to make the enforcement of UK competition law more judicial in character, whether or not private actions are permitted. However, there are several branches of UK law that have been developed relatively recently in which specialist lawyers and judges rapidly acquired the necessary expertise. The Restrictive Practices Court is one example.

On the other hand, there are powerful arguments in favour of allowing private actions. The first is that parties injured by breaches of competition law ought to be able to seek compensation for their losses. At present they can only hope (and lobby?) that the public authorities intervene to stop the damaging practice. Secondly, private parties in some cases have superior information about behaviour that possibly violates competition laws. If private actions were allowed, they would have the incentive and opportunity to use that information, and the public would benefit. Thirdly, the process for selecting cases would be less subject to political (and generally non-economic) influence. Fourthly, there is the prospect that court judgements on private actions would lead to the development of case law, and hence to the greater predictability of competition policy.

To summarize, we have seen that there are considerable differences between the privatized, judicial and adversarial style of US antitrust enforcement, and the nationalized and (mainly) administrative approach in the UK. Competition law in the EEC is in some respects between those two, since it has extensive independent judicial review of the Commission's decisions, and it allows for private actions in the courts of member states. The question of which arrangements are most suitable cannot be divorced from the history, traditions, and wider legal system in each jurisdiction. Subject to that proviso, the organization of competition policy in the EEC has much to commend it.

The Contributed Papers

The previous sections of this chapter have sought to provide the reader with an appraisal of the current state of the art in competition policy in the USA, the UK, and the EEC. We have not hesitated to give our own evaluation of those policies. It was indeed inevitable that we should do so, since there is no consensus on competition policy. Instead there is a vigorous debate, which is reflected in the papers which are published in the rest of this book.

We may identify two causes of the current debate. The first is the increasing involvement of economic analysis in competition policy, coupled with the development in recent years of the sophisticated analytical tools associated with the 'new industrial economics'. The second is a feeling, in the aftermath of major cases in both the US and the EEC, that competition policy is poorly focused, and ill designed to fulfil the objective of improving the market allocation of resources in advanced industrial economies. The conference from which this volume of papers has evolved was called specifically to explore these two elements, and to enquire whether competition policy could, and should, be put on a sounder footing. The brief description of the papers which follows may help the reader to place them in context. It is not, of course, a substitute for a careful reading of them.

The first two papers, by Schmalensee and Phlips, deal primarily with recent developments of industrial economic analysis, in respect of understanding market behaviour. These are then made the basis of critical remarks in respect of the content and practice of competition policy. Schmalensee explores the debate in the literature between two explanations of dominance – rent-seeking and innovation – and concludes that both are consistent with the evidence from different examples. The persistence of dominance is traced particularly to strategic advantages, created and enjoyed by dominant firms, arising from irreversible long-lived investments in tangible or intangible assets, which give rise to credible threats of retaliation against entrants. Turning to policy, Schmalensee highlights the second-best nature of any solutions offered to the problem of dominance. For example, restricting predatory reactions to entry may give firms an incentive to spend more on pre-entry strategic expenditures. Similarly, taking too tough a line on firms that achieve dominance in innovation may have adverse effects on the incentives to undertake R & D. Despite the ambiguity of much welfare analysis of market conduct, he none the less argues the case for rule-based antitrust, rather than a more discretionary rule-of-reason approach.

Phlips addresses the question of policy towards information sharing in oligopolistic industries. He shows that information sharing and parallelism in pricing, which are usually taken to be evidence of tacitly *collusive* behaviour, may also characterize non-cooperative Nash equilibria. It is therefore essential to look more closely at information sharing devices to determine which are collusive and which are not. More controversially, he proposes that the objective of competition policy should be defined in terms of Nash equilibria with zero conjectural variations, rather than the usual criterion of price equals marginal cost. His argument is that this represents a more realistic objective.

The paper by George Hay traces the development of the underlying philosophy of antitrust activity in the United States since 1945. He distinguishes three modes of policy. In the first mode, which lasted up to 1975, antitrust policy in the US was marked by hostility to many forms of market conduct, without regard to market power. This hostility meant that a dominant firm would be attacked if it showed any sign of wanting to compete. Effectively, the only behaviour allowed was to exploit its monopoly position by charging a high price! The second mode was ushered in by the Areeda-Turner paper on predatory pricing in 1975. The proposed definition of predatory pricing now made it possible for a dominant firm to compete on price without necessarily attracting the disapproval of the antitrust authorities. In the third mode, which Hay suggests is just beginning in the US, the focus of policy is narrowed to a scrutiny of the conduct of *dominant* firms alone: non-dominant firms are allowed to do what they like. The point is that in a competitive situation a firm which adopts any market conduct which is inimical to the interests of consumers will find itself losing market share. As an illustration of this third mode, Hay takes the Vertical Restraint Guidelines issued by the US Department of Justice, with their emphasis on a structural screen before a particular market practice is investigated. A particularly valuable aspect of Hay's paper is the use of UK and EEC competition cases to illustrate the way in which these jurisdictions are in modes one and two of policy.

There is, however, a serious problem in the application of a structural screen prior to the investigation of market conduct. This is identified by Hay as the possibility that structure is itself endogenous, the outcome of conduct. The obvious example is the monopolist who fixes a high price, and thereby attracts competition. The appearance of competition may be deceptive. So, in addition, it would seem right to include in the screening process some investigation of reported profit levels. But the practice of analysing accounting profit rates as a guide to economic returns has been strongly criticized, it being asserted that it is quite unreliable.

This pessimism is strongly challenged in the paper by Kay, which shows the conditions under which accounting data can be utilized and interpreted. The long-held belief that high reported profit rates are not entirely unrelated to the economic profitability of the firm is vindicated. That being so, George Hay's proposal that the screening process should include both market share and profitability has much to commend it. It should be emphasized that it is a screening process: it is not a substitute for a careful analysis of conduct once the screen has suggested that the market or firm is worthy of investigation.

The final paper, by Geroski, returns to a theme raised by Schmalensee: do dominant firms decline? The relevance of this theme is obvious. If dominance is a matter for policy concern, then it is important to know how effective are market processes in eliminating it. If dominant positions are eroded rapidly, then the role of policy might be to assist that process. If, on the other hand, dominant positions are maintained over a long period, then the antitrust authorities presumably have a tougher task on their hands. The evidence surveyed by Geroski suggests that the decline of firms with dominant positions is at best extremely slow. Nor is there much convincing evidence that dominant firms themselves accept decline in return for high profits in the short run. This evidence leads him to change the question – to ask instead what are the mechanisms that permit dominant firms to retain their positions over very long periods. The suggested answer is that it is a regular stream of competitive challenges which keeps such firms on their mettle. Without such challenges a firm may become sleepy and eventually succumb. A paradox for policy then emerges: it may be competition, rather than the absence of competition, which sustains a dominant firm's position. The implications for the design of competition policy are far from clear.

References

Abreu, D. 1984: Infinitely repeated games with discounting: a general theory. Princeton University, unpublished paper.

Adams, W. J. and Yellen, J. 1976: Commodity bundling and the burden of monopoly. *Quarterly Journal of Economics*, 90, 475–98.

Areeda, P. and Turner, D. 1975: Predatory pricing and related practices under section 2 of the Sherman Act. *Harvard Law Review*, 88, 667–733.

Bailey, E. E. 1986: Price and productivity change following deregulation: the US experience. *Economic Journal*, 96, 1–17.

Baumol, W. J. 1982: Contestable markets: an uprising in the theory of industry structure. *American Economic Review*, 72, 1–15.

Baumol, W. J. and Klevorick, A. K. 1971: Input choices and rate of return regulation: an overview of the discussion. *Bell Journal of Economics*, 2, 162–90.

Baumol, W. J., Panzar, J. C. and Willig, R. D. 1982: *Contestable Markets and the Theory of Industry Structure*. New York: Harcourt, Brace, Jovanovich.
Brock, G. W. 1975: *The US Computer Industry: a study of market power*. Cambridge, Mass.: Harvard University Press.
Brock, G. W. 1981: *The Telecommunications Industry*. Cambridge, Mass.: Harvard University Press.
Brock, W. A. 1983: Contestable markets and the theory of industry structure: a review article. *Journal of Political Economy*, 91, 1055–66.
Cowling, K. and Mueller, D. 1978: The social costs of monopoly. *Economic Journal*, 88, 727–48.
Cowling, K. and Mueller, D. 1981: The social costs of monopoly power revisited. *Economic Journal*, 91, 721–5.
Dasgupta, P. and Stiglitz, J. 1980: Industrial structure and the nature of innovative activity. *Economic Journal*, 90, 266–93.
Dixit, A.K. and Norman, V. 1978: Advertising and welfare. *Bell Journal of Economics*, 9, 1–17. Reply, 1980, 10, 728–9; another reply, 1980, 11, 753–4.
Dixit, A. K. and Stiglitz, J. E. 1977: Monopolistic competition and optimum product diversity. *American Economic Review*, 67, 297–308.
Fairburn, J., Kay, J. and Sharpe, T. 1984: The economics of Article 86. IFS working paper no. 50.
Firth, M. 1979: The profitability of takeovers and mergers. *Economic Journal*, 89, 316–28.
Friedman, J. 1971: A non-cooperative equilibrium for supergames. *Review of Economics and Statistics*, 28, 1–12.
Fisher, F., McGowan, J. and Greenwood, J. 1983: *Folded, Spindled, and Mutilated: economic analysis and US v. IBM*. Cambridge, Mass.: MIT Press.
Geroski, P. and Jacquemin, A. 1984: Dominant firms and their alleged decline. *International Journal of Industrial Organization*, 2, 1–27.
Gilbert, R. and Newbery, D. 1982: Pre-emptive patenting and the persistence of monopoly. *American Economic Review*, 72, 514–26.
Green, E. and Porter, R. 1984: Non-cooperative collusion under imperfect price information. *Econometrica*, 52, 87–100.
Grossman, S.J. and Hart, O.D. 1980: Takeover bids, the free-rider problem and the theory of the corporation. *Bell Journal of Economics*, 11, 1, 42–64.
Hannah, L. and Kay, J. A. 1977: *Concentration in Modern Industry*. London: Macmillan.
Harberger, A. 1954: Monopoly and resource allocation. *American Economic Review*, 44, 73–87.
Hay, D.A. and Morris, D. J. 1979: *Industrial Economics: theory and evidence*. Oxford: Oxford University Press.
Hay, G. A. 1981: A confused lawyer's guide to the predatory pricing literature. In S. Salop (ed.), *Strategy, Predation and Antitrust Analysis*, Washington DC: Federal Trade Commission.

Hay, G. A. 1985a: Anti-trust and economic theory: some observations from the US experience. *Fiscal Studies*, 6, 59–69.

Hay, G. A. 1985b: Competition policy. *Oxford Review of Economic Policy*, 1, 63–79.

Kahn, A. E. 1971: *The Economics of Regulation*, 2 volumes. New York: Wiley.

Katz, M. 1984a: Price discrimination and monopolistic competition. *Econometrica*, 52, 1453–71.

Katz, M. 1984b: An analysis of cooperative R & D. Princeton discussion paper no. 76.

Katz, M. and Shapiro, C. 1985: Network externalities, competition, and compatibility. *American Economic Review*, 75, 424–40.

Kay, J. A. 1983: A general equilibrium approach to the measurement of monopoly welfare loss. *International Journal of Industrial Organization*, 1, 317–32.

Kay, J. A. and Sharpe, T. 1982: The anticompetitive practice. *Fiscal Studies*, 3, 191–8.

Kay, J. A. and Silberston, Z. A. 1984: The new industrial policy – privatisation and competition. *Midland Bank Review*, Spring.

Klemperer, P. 1984: Collusion via switching costs. Stanford University Graduate School of Business discussion paper no. 786.

Kreps, D., Milgrom, P., Roberts, J. and Wilson, R. 1982: Rational cooperation in a finitely repeated prisoners' dilemma game. *Journal of Economic Theory*, 27, 245–52.

Leibenstein, H. 1966: Allocative efficiency versus X-efficiency. *American Economic Review*, 56, 392–415.

Littlechild, S. C. 1981: Misleading calculations of the social cost of monopoly power. *Economic Journal*, 91, 348–63.

Manne, H. G. 1965: Mergers and the market for corporate control. *Journal of Political Economy*, 73.

Marvel, H. P. and McCafferty, S. 1984: Resale price maintenance and quality competition. *Rand Journal of Economics*, 15, 346–59.

Maskin, E. and Riley, J. 1984: Monopoly with incomplete information. *Rand Journal of Economics*, 15, 171–96.

Masson, R. T. and Shaanan, J. 1984: Social costs of oligopoly and the value of competition. *Economic Journal*, 94, 520–35.

Mathewson, G. F. and Winter, R. A. 1984: An economic theory of vertical restraints. *Rand Journal of Economics*, 15, 27–38.

Meeks, G. 1977: *Disappointing Marriage: a study of the gains from merger*. Cambridge: Cambridge University Press.

Merkin, R. and Williams, K. 1985: *Competition Law: antitrust policy in the United Kingdom and the EEC*. London: Street and Maxwell.

Milgrom, P. and Roberts, J. 1984: Price and advertising signals of product quality. Unpublished paper.

Nelson, P. 1970: Information and consumer behaviour. *Journal of Political Economy*, 78, 311–29.

Neven, D. and Phlips, L. 1985: Discriminating oligopolists and common markets. *Journal of Industrial Economics*, 34, 133–50.

Oi, W. Y. 1971: A Disneyland dilemma: two-part tariffs for a Mickey Mouse monopoly. *Quarterly Journal of Economics*, 85, 77–90.

Ordover, J. and Willig, R. 1985: Antitrust for high-technology industries: assessing research joint ventures and mergers. Princeton discussion paper no. 87.

Oren, S., Smith, S. and Wilson, R. 1983: Competitive nonlinear tariffs. *Journal of Economic Theory*, 29, 49–71.

Phlips, L. 1983: *The Economics of Price Discrimination*. Cambridge: Cambridge University Press.

Posner, R. 1974: Theories of economic regulation. *Bell Journal of Economics*, 5, 335–58.

Salop, S. 1979: Strategic entry deterrence. *American Economic Review P & P*, 335–8.

Salop, S. 1981: *Strategy Predation and Antitrust Analysis*. Washington DC: Federal Trade Commission.

Salop, S. 1985: Practices that (credibly) facilitate oligopoly coordination. In G. F. Mathewson and J. E. Stiglitz (eds), *New Developments in the Analysis of Market Structure*, London: Macmillan.

Schmalensee, R. 1978: Entry deterrence in the ready to eat breakfast cereal industry. *Bell Journal of Economics*, 9, 305–27.

Schmalensee, R. 1981a: Output and welfare implications of monopolistic third-degree price discrimination. *American Economic Review*, 71, 242–7.

Schmalensee, R. 1981b: Monopolistic two-part pricing arrangements. *Bell Journal of Economics*, 12, 445–66.

Schwartz, M. and Reynolds, R. J. 1983: Contestable markets: An uprising in the theory of industry structure: comment. *American Economic Review*, 73, 488–96.

Shapiro, C. 1985: Patent licensing and R & D rivalry. *American Economic Review P & P*, 75, 25–30.

Sharpe, T. 1985: British competition policy in perspective. *Oxford Review of Economic Policy*, 1(3), 80–94.

Shepherd, W. 1984: Contestability vs. competition. *American Economic Review*, 74, 572–87.

Spence, A. M. 1975: Monopoly, quality and regulation. *Bell Journal of Economics*, 6, 417–29.

Spence, A. M. 1976: Product selection, fixed costs and monopolistic competition. *Review of Economic Studies*, 43, 217–35.

Spence, A. M. 1983: Contestable markets and the theory of industry structure: a review article. *Journal of Economic Literature*, 21, 981–90.

Stigler, G. 1971: The theory of economic regulation. *Bell Journal of Economics*, 2, 3–21.

Telser, L. G. 1960: Why should manufacturers want fair trade? *Journal of Law and Economics*, 3, 86–105.

Vickers, J. S. 1985: Strategic competition among the few – some recent developments in the economics of industry. *Oxford Review of Economic Policy*, 1.

Vickers, J. S. and Yarrow, G. 1985: *Privatisation and the Natural Monopolies*. London: Public Policy Centre.

von Weizsäcker, C. 1980: *Barriers to Entry: a theoretical treatment*. Berlin: Springer Verlag.

von Weizsäcker, C. 1984: The costs of substitution. *Econometrica*, 52, 1085–116.

Williamson, O. E. 1968: Economies as an antitrust defense. *American Economic Review*, 58, 18–31.

Willig, R. D. 1976: Consumers' surplus without apology. *American Economic Review*, 66, 589–97.

Yarrow, G. K. 1985: Shareholder protection, compulsory acquisition and the efficiency of the takeover process. *Journal of Industrial Economics*, 34, 3–16.

2

Standards for Dominant Firm Conduct: What can Economics Contribute?

RICHARD SCHMALENSEE

Introduction

In one of the more famous dicta in the Alcoa decision, Judge Learned Hand asserted that 'The successful competitor, having been urged to compete, must not be turned upon when he wins.'[1] There is a good deal of irony in this. Hand found Alcoa to have monopolized, and thus to have violated section 2 of the Sherman Act, even though its conduct would have been lawful had it been less successful. In the US and the EEC, firms that have been successful enough to have attained near-monopoly or dominant market positions are subject to rules of conduct stricter than those applied to other firms.[2] Highly 'successful' firms are thus always 'turned upon' to some extent. As one law professor turned executive puts it, enforcement of the US antitrust laws generally involves 'beating up the winners'.[3]

In this essay I explore the contributions that industrial economics and industrial economists can make to debates about general rules of conduct or case-specific remedies proposed for application to firms that have attained 'dominance'. I limit my attention to considerations of economic efficiency, though antitrust policy may of course be employed to pursue

I am indebted to Ian Ayres, Paul Geroski, Paul Joskow, Garth Saloner, the editors, and the other conference participants for useful comments on an earlier version of this essay. The usual waiver of liability applies, of course.

[1] *US* v. *Aluminum Company of America*, 148 F.2d 416 (1945).

[2] Fox (1984) provides a nice discussion of the cases decided by the EC Court of Justice under article 86 of the Treaty of Rome, and a comparison with US antitrust law.

[3] Remarks of Robert B. Shapiro, in 'Antitrust in transition: two dialogues', the Conference Board, Research Bulletin 184, New York, 1985, p. 21. In the original, oral version of these remarks, the phrase was 'winner-bashing'.

other objectives as well. (Here and in all that follows I use 'antitrust' for what is called 'antitrust' in the US and 'competition law' elsewhere. This correctly signals my much greater familiarity with antitrust policy in the US than elsewhere.)

I begin in the second section by defining market dominance in the antitrust context and discussing the persistence of dominant positions over time. The third section considers theory and historical evidence on the origins of dominant positions.

Relying on this background, the fourth section argues that the efficiency consequences of 'beating up the winners', by imposing rules designed to limit the returns to dominance or to hasten its erosion, are generally unknowable. (Rules aimed at preventing the acquisition of dominant positions are not explicitly considered, though most of the arguments and conclusions advanced here also apply to such rules.) Several fundamental second-best problems are unavoidable when competition is imperfect, and, as usual, second-best problems give rise to policy prescriptions too complex to be followed with any precision. As I have discussed elsewhere (Schmalensee, 1982a), difficulties of this sort that are inherent in many areas of antitrust policy have been made visible by recent theoretical work in industrial economics.

The fifth section considers in general terms what economists *can* contribute to the task of devising efficiency-enhancing rules for dominant firm conduct in the light of these difficulties. While humility is called for, complete agnosticism is not. The academic debate in the US on rules governing predatory pricing and related practices is employed as an illustrative example. The final section provides a brief summary of the essay's main points and their implications for debates in antitrust policy.

Market Dominance and its Persistence

The meanings attached to 'dominant firm' and 'monopoly' in the antitrust context are broader than the definitions of those terms in economic theory. A dominant firm in economic theory is generally a single large seller facing many small price-taking rivals, while a monopoly is the only seller of some good or service. In antitrust policy, both terms are generally used to refer to a seller that is able to exercise substantial market power (or, equivalently, monopoly power) unilaterally, without the need for collusive arrangements. This definition of dominance or monopoly – which I adopt here – includes markets approximating (to an unspecified degree of exactness) the limiting cases of theory. Firms that pass this test are usually appreciably larger than their closest rivals, since tacit or overt collusion is typically required for the exercise of appreciable market power in oligopolistic markets.

As Landes and Posner (1981) argue, economic theory indicates that one ought to define a firm with substantial market power as one that is able to enhance its profits by raising prices substantially above marginal costs for a substantial volume of sales. The deadweight loss produced by the exercise of monopoly power provides a natural measure of substantiality reflecting both of these considerations (Schmalensee, 1982b). Most firms in developed economies have some market power; only a few have enough to be characterized as dominant or as monopolies. There is essentially no basis in economics for the existence of a sharp dividing line between dominant firms and others, however, since market power is measured along a continuum.

Market power is often associated with market share, and judgements about the presence or absence of market power often turn on the definition of the 'relevant market', especially in US antitrust cases. For the purposes of assessing market power, it is logical to follow Areeda and Turner (1978, p. 347) and define a relevant market for antitrust purposes as 'a firm or group of firms which, if unified by agreement or merger, would have market power'. In other words, a market is an aggregation (over space and/or products) of outputs that could profitably be monopolized, at least in the short run. (The smallest such aggregate should generally be the focus of analysis.) This definition is also broadly consistent with the discussions of market definition in Landes and Posner (1981) and the US Department of Justice (1984) Merger Guidelines. Dominant firms commonly have large shares of sales in one or more relevant markets thus defined. But the correspondence between market share and market power is far from exact, and market share is not necessarily the best indicator of power.[4]

In the Cellophane case, the US Supreme Court ruled that under section 2 of the Sherman Act a monopoly is a firm with 'the power to control prices or exclude competition'.[5] This blurs the important distinction between short-run and long-run market power. A seller with a very large share of market capacity or output is likely have considerable *short-run* market power, since it should be able profitably 'to control prices' to an appreciable extent in the short run. Exceptions may arise when the largest

---

[4] These points and the arguments of the next paragraph are developed in Landes and Posner (1981) and Schmalensee (1979, 1982b).

[5] *US* v. *E.I. Dupont de Nemours and Company*, 351 US 377 (1956).

firm has higher costs than its rivals or can only produce inferior products. But *long-run* market power – 'the power to control price' in the face of the investment decisions of actual and potential rivals – *requires* the ability to restrict or 'exclude competition'. And, as the work of Worcester (1957), Gaskins (1971), and others shows, the power to exclude competition in the long run can only derive from long-run (i.e. long-lived) *advantages* over actual or potential rivals. This literature makes it clear that size does not by itself confer such advantages. As Stigler's (1964) discussion of the difficulty of detecting price cuts by small firms indicates, size can even be a strategic handicap (see also Gelman and Salop, 1983).

Salop (1979) has pointed out that there are two types of long-run advantage that may enable an established dominant firm to preserve its market position despite assaults by entrants, who may be newcomers to the industry or aggressive fringe firms. (I depart from Salop's terminology in what follows.) *Operating* advantages correspond to Bain's (1956) absolute cost and product differentiation barriers to entry. A firm with operating advantages has lower costs or more favourable demand conditions (perhaps because of superior products) than any potential entrant. Patents and trade secrets are the most obvious potential sources of such asymmetries. If a dominant firm has operating advantages, it is simply not feasible for an entrant to match its cost/demand position. The entrant would thus be at a disadvantage relative to the incumbent in post-entry operations.

On the other hand, *strategic* advantages may arise in this context simply because the dominant firm appears on the market first and can acquire assets before potential entrants make their decisions. (These are called first-mover advantages in the language of game theory.) In Bain's (1956) analysis, scale economies can provide an incumbent firm with a strategic advantage: even given that products are homogeneous and all firms' costs are given by the same function, if an entrant adds appreciably to industry capacity (so as to avoid being at a cost disadvantage), price may be sufficiently depressed as to render entry unattractive even though incumbents earn substantial excess profits. Strategic advantages arise when an entrant can acquire the same tangible (plant, equipment) and intangible (technology, reputation) assets as an established firm but can only do so on less favourable terms. Unlike operating advantages, strategic advantages are not eroded by the expiration of patents or the diffusion of knowledge among potential entrants. But if successful entry does occur, strategic advantages do not help the incumbent firm in post-entry competition.

As Geroski and Jacquemin (1984) have emphasized in their valuable overview of the relevant theoretical literature, dominant firms may obtain stategic advantages from many sources.[6] Generally these involve the ability of established firms to make irreversible, long-lived investments in tangible or intangible assets before entrants appear. That is, sunk costs (Baumol and Willig, 1981) must be present and important. By incurring sunk costs in a strategic manner, an incumbent may be able to make a *commitment* that makes credible a threat to respond harshly to entry. (A threat is credible if and only if it would be in the interest of the threatener to carry it out; non-credible threats are bluffs. See Dixit, 1982 for a nice exposition of these and related concepts.) Spence (1981a) terms such investments pre-entry *positioning moves*, as opposed to post-entry *reactions* to new entry. As Spence emphasizes, both sorts of actions generally involve a waste of resources, as do entrants' attempts to respond. (On this latter point especially, see Hillman, 1984.)

A second common theme in the literature on strategic advantages is the existence of scale economies of one sort or another, following Bain (1956). Scale economies make it uneconomic for an entrant to appear at such a small scale that no substantial competitive response to its entry would be rational. If such entry is possible, pre-entry market conditions fully describe the post-entry environment.

Spence's (1977) seminal rehabilitation of the concept of entry deterrence furnishes the standard example of strategic advantage and of pre-entry positioning by an established firm. In that paper and the large literature to which it has given rise, an incumbent monopolist faced with the threat of entry rationally makes larger irreversible investments in production capacity than it otherwise would. These socially inefficient investments make vigorous reaction to entry more attractive to the incumbent by lowering its marginal costs for high levels of output. This in turn makes entry less attractive, especially in the presence of scale economies. (Interesting recent contributions to this literature include

[6] Roberts (1985) nicely surveys the most recent theoretical work. I must quarrel with Geroski and Jacquemin's (1984, pp. 3–5) decision to *define* dominance by the presence of strategic advantages. This departs from conventional usage in a potentially confusing direction, since even incumbent firms with very little market power may have strategic advantages over potential entrants; see, for instance, Bernheim (1984), Lane (1980), and Prescott and Visscher (1977).

Bulow et al., 1985a; and Eaton and Lipsey, 1981.) In order for this mechanism to be an important source of persistent dominant firm profits, however, scale economies must be unusually important by US standards (Schmalensee, 1981a).

Pre-entry investment in long-lived capacity is not the only potential source of strategic advantage for dominant firms. In markets in which buyers incur direct or opportunity (Schmalensee, 1982c) costs of switching to new brands, the first firm to make substantial sales acquires a strategic advantage over later entrants, which may serve to deter entry in the presence of scale economies. No inefficient, positioning investment is required to obtain this advantage, though its optimal exploitation may involve sacrificing profits in order to penetrate the market more rapidly than would be optimal if there were no threat of subsequent entry.

In some situations, established dominant firms can rationally make pre-emptive investments that eliminate avenues along which entry might occur. Such investments may involve new products that crowd geographic (Eaton and Lipsey, 1979) or product (Schmalensee, 1978) space. Alternatively, as Gilbert and Newbery (1982) have shown, an incumbent may be able profitably to pre-empt potential new technologies by accelerating its own research and development efforts, even in the absence of scale economies. It is easy to overstate the importance of pre-emptive strategies, however. Pre-emptive investment in R & D, in particular, is possible only under fairly restrictive conditions on the invention/innovation process and the set of potential new technologies.[7]

Advertising may have long-lived effects on buyer behaviour and pre-entry investment in advertising may be a source of stategic advantage. But the competitive effects of such investments depend critically on the way advertising affects buyers; advertising may tilt competition in favour of later entrants under some conditions (Schmalensee, 1983). See Fudenberg and Tirole (1984) and Bulow et al. (1985b) for general discussions of the issues involved.

An incumbent dominant firm's strategic advantages may be rationally exploited by aggressive reactions to entry. It may be rational to engage in

[7] On the conditions necessary for rational pre-emption of technological opportunities see, for instance, Dasgupta (1985), Fudenberg et al. (1983), Harris and Vickers (1985), Lewis (1983), and Reinganum (1983). In an interesting variation on this theme, Gallini (1984) has shown that it may pay an incumbent dominant firm with patent protection to license that patent to a potential entrant (i.e. to permit entry) in order to prevent unprofitable competition to develop a better technology or product. Judd (1985) has recently pointed out some diffculties in making credible pre-emptive investments in new products.

predation to prevent outsiders from matching the established firm's knowledge of cost and demand conditions (Scharfstein, 1984). It may also be rational to engage in predation to build a reputation for toughness that will discourage other potential entrants (Kreps and Wilson, 1982; Milgrom and Roberts, 1982) or facilitate merger on favourable terms (Saloner, 1985). Similarly, a rational incumbent may attempt to eliminate rivals before they have been able to demonstrate their competence to suppliers of capital (Benoit, 1984; Fudenberg and Tirole, 1985). Advertising may rationally be used as a predatory weapon under some conditions (Hilke and Nelson, 1984). And the work of Salop and Scheffman (1983) suggests that established firms may be able credibly to threaten a variety of wasteful, cost-increasing reactions to entry (such as litigation) without making any pre-entry positioning moves.

Finally, the presence of firm-specific (i.e. proprietary) learning economies can create both strategic and operating advantages. (See Spence, 1981b and Fudenberg and Tirole, 1983 for theoretical analyses; and Lieberman, 1984 for interesting evidence on the importance of proprietary learning economies.) An established firm may be able to lower its costs well below those of potential entrants by increasing output before the threat of entry appears. Once it has done this, it has acquired operating advantages. Because later entrants face competition that the first mover did not, they cannot expect to be able to invest in lower costs by increasing output on the same terms that the established dominant firm faced.

Unfortunately, the theoretical prediction that dominant positions not protected by strategic or operating advantages will tend to decay tells us nothing about the speed with which such positions decay in real markets. This is an empirical question. Similarly, even though a large number of strategic and operating advantages can in theory prevent entry indefinitely, one cannot conclude that real dominant positions never decay. In a world in which tastes and technologies change and managements protected from competition tend to go soft, one expects dominant firms' advantages to retard the growth of competition, not to exclude it completely and forever. Moreover, as Caves et al. (1984) emphasize, a dominant firm with weak advantages over actual and potential competitors may choose to accept the inevitability of its own decline and concentrate on maximizing short-run profits, rather than to spend money to deter potential new entrants or to discourage aggressive rivals. A second empirical question is then the importance of the strategic and operating advantages discussed in the theoretical literature in preventing or retarding the decay of dominance in real industries.

Most studies of the evolution of dominant positions do not focus clearly on either of these questions. Weiss and Pascoe (1984) have argued that dominance has tended to persist in recent years, for instance, and Mueller (1977) has argued that interfirm profitability differences also persist over long periods, but neither paper tells us why. (See also Geroski's paper in this volume and the references he cites on the persistence of large market shares.) A study of the evolution of firms with large market shares created by mergers in the US between 1882 (Standard Oil) and 1903 (the Northern Securities decision) seems a very promising source of answers. A contemporary observer identified 78 large mergers in this period resulting in firms controlling at least half the output of their industries.[8]

For instance, if one assumes that US Steel had no long-run advantages over its rivals (see note 10 below; and Chandler, 1977, p. 361), the decline in its market share from 66 per cent in 1901 to 42 per cent in 1925 (Stigler, 1965) may be taken as suggestive of a half-life of purely short-run dominance of about 37 years.[9] This seems very slow decay indeed, and Geroski's analysis in this volume suggests that it is not unusual. But, as Caves et al. (1984) note, a sizeable number of apparently dominant firms formed in the same merger movement failed within a few years of their creation (see Chandler, 1977, chapter 10 for a discussion of some examples). Caves and his associates study 34 large mergers that survived until 1929, and they present evidence that firms with weak advantages suffered more rapid declines in market share than others but enjoyed higher profits. They attribute this pattern to rational decisions to harvest weakly protected dominant positions even if entry was thereby accelerated.

Overall, the pattern that emerges is mixed. Some firms that apparently began with dominant positions vanished quickly: the National Cordage Association failed three years after its formation (Chandler, 1977, pp. 329–30). But some firms created around the turn of the century remained dominant for a half-century or more: consider Eastman Kodak and United Shoe Machinery. Market dominance is not inevitably long lived but, if it is protected by substantial and continuing operating or strategic advantages, it may persist for many decades.

[8] J. Moody, *The Truth about the Trusts* (Moody, New York, 1904), p. 487; cited in Stigler (1950). For overviews of these 'mergers for monopoly', as Stigler calls them, and the associated early literature, see also Caves et al. (1984) and Chandler (1977).

[9] Suppose the share decays exponentially, with the share t years after formation given by $S(t) = S(0)\exp(-kt)$. Setting $S(0) = 0.66$ and $S(24) = 0.42$, one obtains $k = 0.0188$, which implies $S(36.9) = S(0)/2$.

Sources of Market Dominance

Restrictions on the conduct of dominant firms limit the returns to the activity of creating market dominance. The literature contains two competing characterizations of this activity. The first follows Posner (1975) and emphasizes rent-seeking, while the second follows Schumpeter (1942) and stresses innovation.

Posner (1975) argued that there are no barriers to entry to the business of creating monopolies, so that the average returns to this activity should be competitive. (One might think about the business of increasing concentration through horizontal mergers in this context.) If, as he contended, this activity is not itself directly productive, one would expect that on average the present value of the profits of new monopolies should equal the costs expended in competing for their ownership. That is, the rents produced by monopoly should be fully dissipated in the activity of monopoly creation. If this is correct, the social costs of monopoly may be very large indeed; see Cowling and Mueller (1978) for some estimates for the US and the UK.

There are two basic problems with this view, however. First, the assumption of full dissipation is likely to be too strong. Rents will not be fully dissipated if risks and risk aversion are important (Hillman and Katz, 1984) or if competition for monopoly ownership is imperfect (Tullock, 1980). The latter point seems particularly relevant. While everybody would like to own a dominant firm, historically it is hard to find evidence of vigorous competition for many dominant positions. The number of people in a position to contemplate consolidation of the US steel industry in 1901 could not have been large; the number who both recognized the potential gains and expended resources to secure them must have been much smaller. In fact, no evidence of any competition for this particular opportunity is apparent to the reader of the standard secondary sources.

A second problem with the rent-seeking/rent-dissipation view is raised by Demsetz (1976). Posner's (1975) paper and the literature to which it has given rise concentrate on attempts to use the government to create dominant positions. Here one can find evidence of competition through lobbying and other means, though that competition may often be imperfect. (It is presumably no accident that Lyndon Johnson's relatives were granted lucrative rights to operate several television stations in Texas while he was majority leader of the US Senate.) But most dominant positions are not critically dependent on legislation or administrative decisions. In those cases, Demsetz asks, in what socially unproductive, rent-seeking activities can would-be monopolists invest? At the very least, the literature contains no documented examples of substantial investments of this sort unconnected with attempts to influence government decisions. This goes mainly to the question of rent dissipation, of course; horizontal mergers for monopoly may be directly unproductive but require small (net) investments and thus be highly profitable.

Demsetz (1976) gives a Schumpeterian answer to his own question. He contends that would-be monopolists invest in building better mousetraps and that actual monopolists are those who succeed. And one can certainly find examples of apparently dominant firms whose initial market positions derived in large measure from innovation: Alcoa, Gillette, Eastman Kodak, and Xerox come quickly to mind. But this purely Schumpeterian view is incomplete as an empirical matter, and it has no rigorously defensible welfare implications. The promoters of the US Steel merger were surely not engaged in innovative activity in any usual sense of that term. And, while IBM's rise to dominance in the business segment of the mainframe computer market did require innovation, it was certainly facilitated by that firm's prior market position in punched card tabulating machines and by its rivals' early mistakes. Finally, on the normative front, a large literature has now made it clear that Schumpeterian competition can lead to technical progress that is sometimes faster and sometimes slower than the optimum.

Chandler's (1977) study of the origins of large US firms in the years before World War I suggests that on balance innovation, broadly defined, played an important part in the creation of persistent dominant positions in the US. His thesis is basically that innovations in transportation and communications in the nineteenth century created potential economies of scale in some industries and made new forms of production and distribution attractive in others. Some large firms arose because innovative entrepreneurs saw these opportunities and sought to take advantage of them; the large railways, Swift, Montgomery Ward, and Sears provide clear examples. Other large enterprises were created by mergers because existing cartels were perceived as suboptimal or, after 1897, illegal. Examples here include Standard Oil, National Cordage, and National Lead. Chandler discusses many intermediate cases that involved both response to new opportunities and avoidance of competition.

Chandler (1977, pp. 337–44) goes on to argue that successful consolidations (as measured by profitability) generally had two common features. First, they took place 'in the high-volume, large-batch, or continuous process industries and in those needing specialized marketing services' (p. 338), that is, in the industries in which technical change had created new opportunities. Secondly, he contends that 'mergers were rarely successful until managerial hierarchies were created – that is, until production was consolidated and until the firm had its own marketing and purchasing organizations' (p. 338).[10] A central argument of Chandler's book is that the creation of managerial hierarchies was generally an act of innovation in this period, and it was certainly directly productive. Large firms created in industries where there were no scale economies tended to perform badly, especially if managerial hierarchies were not created to impose effective central direction. On the other hand, scale economies were sometimes exploited to produce strategic advantages that protected dominant positions for decades.

Though Chandler's main focus is on the US, his central arguments have to do with the consequences of technical change, not with US institutions. Thus his work is at least suggestive about the creation and evolution of market dominance outside the US. On the other hand, for various reasons, horizontal mergers seem to have played a greater role in the creation and maintenance of dominant positions in other countries; see, for instance, Hannah and Kay (1977). This may well reflect more rent-seeking activity.

The discussion here and in the previous section leads to the following view of the positive economics of market dominance, which I adopt in what follows. Firms may achieve short-run dominance through merger or other actions that are not directly productive. But most dominant positions, particularly those created in the US after 'merger for monopoly' was ruled illegal in 1903, have their origins to an important extent in innovation, broadly defined. Firms that attain short-run dominance by merger or other means but have no advantages over actual and potential rivals and are badly managed tend to perform poorly and lose dominance in a matter of years. In other cases, dominant positions

[10] The US Steel merger seems an exception to this generalization. It occurred in the right sort of industry and was clearly successful (Stigler, 1965). In Chandler's (1977, p. 342) tabular analysis of mergers, he describes the firm as 'integrated', but he notes later (p. 361) that until the 1930s US Steel 'continued to be a holding company that administered its many subsidiaries through a very small general office', which 'did little to coordinate, plan, and evaluate for [sic] the activities of the subsidiaries'. The firm thus 'remained little more than a legal consolidation'. Since production was not rationalized and control was not centralized, it is hard to imagine that US Steel had operating advantages over its rivals or was capable of exploiting any strategic advantages it may have possessed.

may take many decades to decay appreciably, especially if strategic or operating advantages can be exploited by pre-entry positioning moves or post-entry reactions. In the presence of such advantages, the rate of decay of its market position is to some extent under a dominant firm's control; it can sacrifice current profits to slow the erosion of its market share.

Restrictions on Conduct and Second-best Problems

In the light of the foregoing, I now outline some basic problems encountered by attempts to devise efficiency-enhancing restrictions on the conduct of dominant firms. The fundamental point here is that, in imperfectly competitive markets, one must generally solve second-best problems in order to derive efficiency-enhancing rules or remedies.

Classically, second-best problems arise because the impact of changes in one market is affected by distortions in other markets. Thus if the price of oil is above (social) marginal cost, the optimal price of coal is given by a complex formula that is unlikely to describe the result of unregulated competition. Antitrust analysts typically duck problems of this sort (see for instance, Scherer, 1980, pp. 28–9), and I will follow suit. But recent theoretical work in industrial economics has made clear the existence of serious *single-market* second-best problems that are harder to duck. That is, if one or more of the necessary conditions for perfect competition is violated in the coal market, it may not be optimal to move toward satisfaction of any of the other necessary conditions in that market. In this section I outline some of the single-market second-best problems that arise in connection with the antitrust treatment of market dominance.

Let us initially ignore the *long-run* effects of antitrust policy on activities aimed at the creation of dominance. I term the effects that remain *short-run* for simplicity, though it should be clear from the discussion above that the short run can be very long indeed by usual standards.

Consider first rules aimed at limiting the exploitation of a dominant firm's market power. The clearest case for short-run efficiency gains is provided by the doctrine under article 86 of the Treaty of Rome that high prices can constitute abuse of a dominant position. (See Fox, 1984 for a discussion of (and an American reaction to) the relevant EC Court of Justice cases.) The implicit rule or restriction is that a dominant firm's prices cannot be 'too high'. Putting aside the costs of comprehensive price regulation by non-specialists of firms in many different sectors and ignoring possible multiple-market second-best problems, the short-run efficiency properties of this rule are clear. Society as a whole gains if monopoly prices are reduced, as long as they are not below marginal cost.

Other rules with this same aim have less predictable effects on economic efficiency, however. Limits on price discrimination may reduce the returns to dominance, but the welfare effects of prohibiting classic third-degree price discrimination or tying arrangements used to implement second-degree discrimination (via two-part tariffs) are ambiguous (see Varian, 1985 and Schmalensee, 1981b, respectively). Similarly, limitations on the ability of firms with market power to impose restrictions on their customers may enhance or reduce economic efficiency in theory, and economists have recently come to believe that reductions are more likely. (It should be noted that one cannot easily explain this shift of opinion by pointing to new evidence.) Overstreet's (1983) careful analysis of vertical price-fixing, wherein a manufacturer sets retail prices, reveals the multitude of conflicting theories and bits of evidence that constitute the state of knowledge in the area of vertical restrictions.

Rules designed to hasten the erosion of dominant positions by facilitating new entry or the expansion of fringe firms have been shown to have similarly ambiguous consequences for economic efficiency. As von Weizsäcker (1980a, 1980b) has argued, barriers to entry that (following Bain's 1956 definition) permit established firms to earn supra-competitive profits are not necessarily inefficient when all the conditions necessary for classical perfect competition are not present. A reduction in entry barriers may result in a loss of efficiency.

This is easiest to demonstrate when the persistence of dominance rests in part on operating advantages. Elimination of such advantages in order to facilitate entry may replace low-cost monopoly by high-cost competition. Following Williamson's (1968) pioneering treatment of this problem, suppose that a market with a linear demand curve is served by a monopolist with constant unit cost C that charges a price P. Suppose that antitrust policy can eliminate the dominant firm's advantage and produce a competitive market with price and unit cost equal to $C' > C$. Then some algebra shows that net welfare (consumers' surplus plus producers' profits) increases if and only if

$$C' < (2 - 3^{1/2})P + (3^{1/2} - 1)C = 0.268\,P + 0.732\,C = P(1 - 0.732\,L) \qquad (1)$$

where $L = (P - C)/P$ is the Lerner measure of the (original) degree of monopoly.

As Williamson stressed, a price reduction ($C' < P$) is necessary but not sufficient for a welfare gain. The stronger is the original monopoly position, as measured by L, the greater is the price reduction required to offset the elimination of operating advantages. Condition (1) is a simple formula, but it is hard to imagine antitrust authorities having sufficient information to implement it in particular cases without a substantial chance of error. It is even harder to see how (1) could be used as the basis for a general rule to be applied to all dominant firms.

Even if a dominant firm's operating advantages are untouched, anti-trust policy that facilitates entry may reduce efficiency. Suppose that a dominant firm's position is as above and that there is a single potential entrant with constant unit cost C', with $C < C' < P$. If the second firm enters and post-entry behaviour is Cournot, competition is increased and price is reduced. But, following Schmalensee (1976), efficiency is enhanced under these assumptions if and only if

$$C' < (5/11)P + (6/11)C = 0.455P + 0.545C = P(1 - 0.545L) \qquad (2)$$

This imposes a less stringent test than (1). Higher values of C' are consistent with increased efficiency even though the post-entry price exceeds C' in Cournot equilibrium.

Somewhat surprisingly, a test of intermediate stringency emerges when the queue of potential entrants is long. That is, suppose that N firms enter with cost C' under the assumptions above. Then as N increases without bound, price falls to C' and the condition for welfare improvement is

$$C' < (1/3)P + (2/3)C = 0.333\,P + 0.667\,C = P(1 - 0.667L) \qquad (3)$$

This is less stringent than (1) because the low-cost firm is still producing; it is more stringent than (2) because the low-cost firm has a smaller market share in the limiting equilibrium.

Conditions (2) and (3) would be even more difficult than (1) to apply in particular cases or in the design of general rules, since the number and costs of potential entrants are likely to be very difficult to estimate accurately. Conditions (2) and (3) make clear that privately profitable high-cost entry may be socially inefficient when competition is imperfect. Policies that encourage such entry may therefore reduce economic efficiency, even though they hasten the erosion of dominant positions.

Economies of scale or learning rule out market equilibria or efficient outcomes with many sellers and thus force analysis into the realm of the second best. A number of authors, including von Weizsäcker (1980a,

1980b), Perry (1984), and Mankiw and Whinston (1985), have shown that if established firms lack operating advantages and take no actions to exploit strategic advantages to deter entry, *too much* entry generally occurs when scale economies are present. This occurs because potential entrants do not take into account the fact that their entry would raise the costs and lower the profits of existing firms. That is, even though economies of scale give rise to Bainian entry barriers, entry is likely to be excessive rather than deficient from the viewpoint of economic efficiency. Antitrust policy that prevents the exploitation of strategic advantages or otherwise facilitates entry may reduce efficiency under these conditions, even though it enhances competition and reduces wasteful investment in pre-entry positioning. And von Weizsäcker (1980a) has argued that Bainian entry barriers may contribute to social efficiency in other settings as well.

Still restricting attention to the short-run effects of rules designed to facilitate entry in order to erode dominant positions, I mention two additional problems. First, Spence (1981a) has noted that restrictions on permissible reactions to entry, which are the most frequently discussed antimonopoly rules in the US, may not in fact prevent dominant firms from deterring entry. Such restrictions may instead cause dominant firms to increase the resources they devote to pre-entry positioning moves. Such investments are generally wasteful, as are potential entrants' attempts to offset them (Hillman, 1984). But, as Spence (1981a, p. 60) points out, 'there are no known, unambiguously beneficial, simple rules that can be applied to investments prior to entry.' That is, positioning is even harder to regulate efficiently than reactions. Second, Bernheim (1984) has shown that when potential entrants appear sequentially over time, policies that make entry deterrence more difficult may have the perverse effect of discouraging entry on balance. If tomorrow's entry cannot be deterred, today's entry may not occur.

I have argued so far that, aside from regulation that forces monopoly prices closer to marginal costs, it is hard to find rules designed to limit the ability of dominant firms to exploit their market positions that are unambiguously efficiency enhancing in the short run. And it may be even more difficult to design rules that will both hasten the erosion of dominant positions and improve economic welfare in the short run. The use of strategic and (especially) operating advantages to deter entry is not necessarily socially undesirable. When we consider the long-run effects of restrictions on dominant firm conduct, a new set of difficulties appears, and even the efficiency properties of price ceilings are seen to be unclear in principle.

Rules that limit the short-run returns to dominant positions or hasten their erosion reduce the attractiveness of investments aimed at producing market dominance. If all such investments represented directly unproductive rent-seeking, such rules would be efficiency enhancing on this score.

But, as I argued in the previous section, life is not so simple. Many dominant positions are at least in part attributable to innovative activity, broadly defined. Policies that reduce the present value of market dominance thus reduce the returns to innovation. Despite the importance of innovation in advancing economic welfare, however, it does not follow that all restrictions on dominant firms have undesirable long-run effects. Reductions in patent lifetimes also reduce the returns to innovation, but it does not follow that the optimal patent lifetime is infinite. And, despite Schumpeter's (1942) eloquence, there is no good reason to think that unrestricted market competition produces the optimal rate and direction of technical progress.

The patent analogy is both instructive and depressing. Attempts to deduce the optimal patent lifetime serve mainly to make clear the intractable nature of this problem. (See Nordhaus, 1969 for the most important attempt at its solution; Scherer, 1977, pp. 25–34 surveys the literature.) Again we are in the realm of the second best; longer patent lifetimes encourage innovation but prolong monopoly. A host of clearly arbitrary special assumptions are required to produce a quantitative 'solution'. The analogous problem of the optimal degree of severity of restrictions on dominant firms is even less tractable, for two reasons. First, while innovative activity may be an important source of dominant positions, it is plainly not the only source. To an unknown extent, restrictions on dominant firms also lower the returns to directly unproductive rent-seeking. Secondly, there is no single variable in the dominant firm context that corresponds directly to patent lifetime. Antitrust policy is multidimensional and cannot reliably dictate the lifetimes of dominant firms.

When the long-run effects of restrictions on dominant firms are considered, then, the ambiguity revealed by short-run analysis deepens. In particular, restrictions on the level of prices charged by dominant firms are no longer clearly efficiency enhancing. Even if patents are not involved, such restrictions are likely to reduce the returns to innovation, broadly defined.

I must admit that this long-run analysis strikes even its author as somewhat academic in the context of current antitrust policies in the US and

Western Europe. The gains to entrepreneurs and/or shareholders from creating an enterprise like Xerox or IBM are currently so enormous that it is hard to believe that even a sizeable percentage reduction in those rewards would have much effect on innovative activity. But this is purely an opinion; I know of no hard evidence that could be used to make it into a rigorous argument.

Potential Contributions of Economics and Economists

The preceding analysis is depressing stuff for an economist interested in antitrust policy. The arguments of the previous section imply that such an economist can never hope to prove that any proposed general rule restricting dominant firm conduct would increase or decrease efficiency in all cases. Further, contemplation of the unusually simple rules presented in the previous section, in the light of the state of empirical knowledge in industrial economics, suggests that it will rarely be possible to support rigorously an assertion that any proposed general rule will enhance efficiency in most cases or that the costs of adopting (or not adopting) it will outweigh the benefits. Moreover, second-best problems make it nearly impossible to analyse rigorously and completely the efficiency consequences of many sorts of case-specific rules, even if long-run effects are ignored.

Recognition of these problems should make us a bit more humble than many economists have been or seemed to be in the past. But I do not think that we need to be absolutely silent in debates about general rules or particular cases. In this section I present three principles that economists can use to make positive contributions to antitrust policies toward dominant firms, and I illustrate my general remarks with a brief discussion of the US debate on predatory practices. (For a broadly similar sermon, addressed by a US law professor (now judge) to his peers, see Easterbrook, 1984.)

First, *rules designed to 'beat up the winners' should only be applied to genuine winners.* That is to say, rules that have as their main rationale their ability to reduce the value of dominant positions or to hasten their demise should only be applied to dominant firms – sellers with unusually important monopoly power. This simple observation has implications for both rule-making and the analysis of particular cases.

In the US, for instance, rules against tying contracts and price discrimination apply, in principle at least, to firms with small amounts of

market power (Landes and Posner, 1981). Since the efficiency properties
of these restrictions on conduct are unclear if market structure is taken as
given, it is not apparent why they should be imposed upon non-dominant
sellers without much monopoly power. If a firm has little monopoly
power, the potential gains from limiting the returns to that power or
hastening its erosion are correspondingly small. On the other hand, the
efficiency case against applying these rules to dominant firms is less
clear, since they may serve to alter market structures in a procompetitive
direction. But if such a tax on dominance is imposed, it should clearly be
accompanied by an economically valid test for dominance. Economists
have a good deal to say about such tests (see my second section) and
about their application to particular cases. The same progress in
industrial economics that has weakened our confidence in normative
prescriptions has strengthened our ability to diagnose market power.

Secondly, I think that *the efficiency effects of proposed general rules
or case-specific remedies should be debated*, even if economists cannot
analyse them completely and rigorously. Two plausible presumptions
can serve to structure such debates.

On the one hand, in the light of the many virtues of the market mechanism, general rules or case-specific remedies that would alter the outcome of market processes ought not to be adopted unless supported by a
plausible argument that short-run efficiency (in the sense of the previous
section) is likely to be enhanced, even if the overall long-run net effect
must remain unknowable. This presumption, for instance, suggests that
the burden of proof should be borne by those who would prevent dominant firms from engaging in business practices that are not uncommon
among non-dominant firms; their use by such firms would seem to create
a rebuttable presumption that they contribute to efficiency.

On the other hand, a generally procompetitive antitrust policy seems
more likely to enhance efficiency than a policy aimed at any alternative
well-defined objective, and government intervention without well-
defined objectives is likely mainly to produce mischief. I would
accordingly contend that there should also be a rebuttable presumption
that increasing the effectiveness of competition is likely to increase economic efficiency, as long as promoting competition is clearly distinguished
from protecting competitors.[11] It follows from this, for instance, that the
argument that purely punitive measures taken against dominant firms
might in theory increase welfare by reducing rent-seeking should not
serve to rationalize the imposition of such measures.

I think the preceding two paragraphs give a fair description of the
approach most economists (in the US at least) in fact apply to antitrust

issues. The only real novelty here is the explicit recognition that this approach is *not at all* the same thing as rigorous analysis of economic efficiency. A responsible expert in the public arena should not claim too much for his expertise. And we must recognize that the state of our knowledge is such that competent economists will continue to disagree as to the plausibility of efficiency arguments and the likelihood of enhanced competition, both in general and in particular cases. Moreover, the two presumptions advanced above are not fully consistent; they treat differently business practices that are likely to contribute both to the efficiency of a dominant firm's operations and to the preservation of its market position. Competent economists will also continue to disagree about the relative values of operating efficiency and enhanced competition in such contexts.

This second principle is weak in a number of senses. But it can be quite powerful in some situations. It requires that arguments about efficiency and competitive effects be presented and critically evaluated before intervention in market processes is supported. And it is not hard to find examples of antitrust rules or decisions for which no remotely plausible efficiency or competitive arguments exist; the differential treatment of price and non-price vertical restrictions in US antitrust law comes immediately to mind.

Thirdly, *economists should take seriously the social value of predictable rules of law.* The less predictable are antitrust decisions, the more risk is borne by society as a whole, and risk-bearing and risk-shedding actions are socially expensive. If industrial economics generally permitted clear efficiency conclusions to be drawn from rule-of-reason analysis of particular cases, the value of predictability might be overshadowed by the errors that would result from the application of simple, bright-line standards. But in many situations involving dominant firms, the most careful, long, and expensive studies imaginable of the efficiency consequences of particular rules will not produce definitive answers. One knows in advance that competent economists will continue to disagree

[11] Easterbrook (1984) and Leffler (1985) discuss the difficulty of proving, especially to judges and juries, that particular rules or remedies are likely to enhance efficiency. They basically conclude that vigorous competition should replace economic efficiency as the standard for evaluating antitrust proposals. I am broadly sympathetic to this general position and to much of their discussions of its implications. But I think Leffler errs badly when he essentially equates (p. 385) injury to competition with injury to competitors. Investments that lower the costs of a dominant firm generally injure its competitors, but it makes no sense to outlaw cost reduction for this reason.

even after a long and well-run trial and/or the publication of a barrage of articles in the journals.

The alternative is to limit the scope of antitrust proceedings to issues that can be reliably decided and to employ simple general rules as extensively as possible. Rules in the US against price-fixing and horizontal mergers for monopoly permit short proceedings and probably (but not demonstrably) enhance efficiency. To replace them by rule-of-reason standards would make antitrust litigation more expensive and antitrust decisions less predictable, and it is hard to believe that economic efficiency would be enhanced on balance. Economists can speak confidently (if not unanimously) on issues of monopoly power and effects on competition; these can be part of relatively simple rules for deciding antitrust cases. But this leaves us well short of classic, unstructured rule-of-reason proceedings. Indeed, a currently popular prescription with which I generally agree is to move toward 'structured rules of reason' – short algorithms for making decisions about specific allegations. (See the discussion of predatory pricing below.)

As in macroeconomics, we should take seriously the implications of our inability to engage in useful fine-tuning of economic processes. In contrast to macroeconomics, however, there is no new body of theory suggesting that it is impossible in principle to improve on unregulated imperfectly competitive markets. That is, the argument for predictability and simplicity is *not* an argument for *laissez-faire*. It simply implies that attempting to attain unattainable precision is likely to be expensive, both directly and indirectly, and that antitrust authorities should, like Ulysses, tie themselves to the mast to avoid temptation. It is important to note that the result of such an approach may be either softer or tougher than the status quo; it all depends on the sort of rules and procedures that are adopted.

When competent economists disagree on the best simple antitrust rule in a particular context, society may in many circumstances risk little by using predictability and administrative simplicity to settle the argument. But if antitrust policy is to be coherent, and concerned with its natural objective of economic efficiency, the scope for non-economic evidence in antitrust proceedings must be limited. Antitrust decisions should be based primarily on general presumptions or case-specific arguments about competition and efficiency; other considerations should come into play only as tie-breakers.

The debate in the US on optimal antitrust rules to cover 'predatory pricing' and related reactions to entry by dominant firms can serve to illustrate the application of these three principles. This debate was triggered by Areeda and Turner (1975).[12] They noted that prices below short-run marginal cost could not be profit maximizing, were too low from the point of (very) short-run economic efficiency, and could serve to eliminate new sources of competition. They contended that short-run average variable cost was the best available proxy for short-run marginal cost. (I think it would have been better to argue that short-run average variable cost is likely to be the best available proxy for the estimate of short-run marginal cost used by decision-makers.) These arguments led them to propose that a dominant firm found to have set prices below short-run average variable cost in response to entry should be found in violation of section 2 of the Sherman Act. I find the efficiency argument underlying this proposal plausible and thus consistent with the second principle above, though, as Scherer (1976) and others have pointed out, the Areeda-Turner analysis is hardly complete or rigorous.

Scherer (1976) advocated replacing the simple bright-line Areeda-Turner test by a full-blown, efficiency-oriented, unstructured, rule-of-reason analysis of cases involving allegations of predation. If I thought that such analyses were likely to be worth more on average than they would cost, I would agree. The Areeda-Turner rule is surely likely to produce inefficient outcomes in a non-trivial fraction of all predation cases. But Scherer's own description of the factors that would have to be considered in a complete rule-of-reason analysis convinces me that the incremental costs are likely to dwarf the incremental benefits, especially when account is taken of the greater risk that such a process would impose on dominant firms and on both actual and potential entrants. (See also the response by Areeda and Turner, 1976.) If one attaches any substantial value to simplicity and predictability, one must apply the third principle above and reject Scherer's proposal.

Baumol (1979) and Williamson (1977) have proposed alternative tests for predation that do not involve comparing post-entry prices with costs. Their tests involve restricting the *changes* that a dominant firm can make in its pricing in response to the entry or exit of rivals. The welfare argu-

[12] The relevant literature includes contributions by Areeda and Turner (1975, 1976), Baumol (1979), Joskow and Klevorick (1979), Ordover and Willig (1981), Posner (1976), Scherer (1976), Schmalensee (1979), Schwartz (1984), Williamson (1977), and others. For a nice overview of this literature and a discussion of some key cases, see the opinion of Judge Stephen Breyer, *Barry Wright Corp.* v. *ITT Grinnell Corp. et al.*, US Court of Appeals for the First Circuit, 29 December 1983 (reprinted in Commerce Clearing House, *Trade Cases, 1984–1*, pp. 67 252–63).

ment underlying both proposals is that limiting a firm's reaction to entry forces it to lower its pre-entry prices if it wishes to discourage entry, and, since large-scale entry is relatively rare in most industries, pre-entry prices are more important than post-entry prices. This too is plausible. But I think adoption of either proposal would lead to much more complex and uncertain litigation than would variants of the Areeda-Turner rule (see the case-specific discussion in Schmalensee, 1979). I would thus accept weaker efficiency arguments to gain simplicity in this instance, though clearly this is a personal and debatable choice.

Another variant of the Areeda-Turner approach is that of Posner (1976), who argues plausibly that there is no efficiency case for ruling any prices above average total cost illegal. This is not a fully rigorous argument, of course; conditions (2) and (3) above make it clear that if a dominant firm has operating advantages, a price above average total cost can be below the cost of an entrant whose successful entry would be socially beneficial. (See also Roberts, 1985 and the literature he cites on the proposition that successful and socially undesirable predation need not involve sales below cost.) But, as there is no real hope of incorporating conditions like (2) or (3) in a general rule, Posner's proposal seems sensible.

Joskow and Klevorick (1979) have argued for a two-tier approach, in which the courts would throw out cases in which the structural conditions were not conducive to rational and effective predation before applying any cost test. This is perfectly consistent with the first of the principles discussed above; rules aimed at dominant firms in principle should only be applied to dominant firms in practice. It also applies the second principle by limiting the application of rules against predation to situations in which predation might serve to inhibit the erosion of dominant positions.

The argument so far suggests the beginnings of a structured rule-of-reason approach to predation cases. First, apply the first-tier Joskow-Klevorick test, and dismiss any cases not involving dominant firms operating in markets in which predation could be anticompetitive. Secondly, dismiss cases involving prices above the dominant firm's average total cost. Thirdly, rule prices below short-run average variable cost illegal. This leaves a sizeable grey area, involving prices between average total cost and short-run variable cost. In the light of all that has been written on this topic, it seems unlikely that economists will soon agree on the best treatment of such prices.

It follows that simplicity and, possibly, other considerations should be invoked to devise rules governing dominant firms that price between short-run average variable cost and average total cost in response to an entrant. Ordover and Willig (1981), for instance, define predation as actions that would not be profitable unless they had the effect of eliminating a rival. They call this 'an economic definition', but it plainly reflects the dictionary definition of predation and basic notions of fairness rather a rigorous analysis of economic efficiency. (See, for instance, demonstrations by Saloner, 1985 and Schwartz, 1984 that application of this definition may reduce efficiency.) But this is not really a serious criticism to my mind. If one feels that the rules that Ordover and Willig derive from their definition (and the derivation is 'economic' even if the definition is not) were simple and did not conflict with anything in the preceding paragraph, society would likely lose little by adopting them. (I am not personally persuaded that their rules pass these tests, however.)

Conclusions and Implications

Economists have produced a great deal of interesting theory about the nature, origins, and persistence of market dominance. Our factual knowledge is much less systematic and impressive. We know that strategic advantages, unrelated to operating efficiencies, can retard the erosion of market dominance, but it is not clear how important this mechanism is in practice. We know that dominant positions may derive from rent-seeking and from innovation, but we do not know much about the typical mix. Moreover, the more carefully we study economic efficiency questions in markets that have dominant firms (or are imperfectly competitive for other reasons), the more complex are the second-best problems we encounter.

All of this should make us humble about our ability to prescribe efficiency-enhancing general antitrust rules or case-specific remedies. But I do not think that it should reduce economists to silence in this area – even if one could imagine such an outcome. While our ability to deal with questions of economic efficiency and competitive effectiveness is limited, nobody else can do better. If the only effect of economists' contributions to antitrust policy debates were to promote efficiency and competition as goals, we would make a substantial contribution. An active antitrust policy without clear objectives can be a major source of social risk and wasted resources. And, as I have argued in this essay, economists can contribute more than this without sacrificing objectivity or shedding the humility to which we are so richly entitled.

RICHARD SCHMALENSEE

References

Areeda, P. and Turner, D. 1975: Predatory pricing and related practices under section 2 of the Sherman Act. *Harvard Law Review*, 88, 697–733.

Areeda, P. and Turner, D. 1976: Scherer on predatory pricing: a reply. *Harvard Law Review*, 89, 891–8.

Areeda, P. and Turner, D. 1978: *Antitrust Law III*. Boston: Little, Brown.

Bain, J. 1956: *Barriers to New Competition*. Cambridge, Mass.: Harvard University Press.

Baumol, W. 1979: Quasi-permanence of price reduction: a policy for prevention of predatory pricing. *Yale Law Journal*, 89, 1–26.

Baumol, W. and Willig, R. 1981: Fixed costs, sunk costs, entry barriers, public goods, and the sustainability of monopoly. *Quarterly Journal of Economics*, 96, 405–31.

Benoit, J.-P. 1984: Financially constrained entry in a game with incomplete information. *Rand Journal of Economics*, 15, 490–9.

Bernheim, B. D., 1984: Strategic deterrence of sequential entry into an industry. *Rand Journal of Economics*, 15, 1–11.

Bulow, J. I., Geanakoplos, J. D. and Klemperer, P. D. 1985a: Holding idle capacity to deter entry. *Economic Journal*, 95, 178–82.

Bulow, J. I., Geanakoplos, J. D. and Klemperer, P. D. 1985b: Multimarket oligopoly: strategic substitutes and complements. *Journal of Political Economy*, 93, 488–511.

Caves, R., Fortunato, M. and Ghemawat, P. 1984: The decline of dominant firms, 1905–29. *Quarterly Journal of Economics*, 99, 523–46.

Chandler, A. D., Jr 1977: *The Visible Hand: the managerial revolution in American business*. Cambridge, Mass.: Harvard University Press.

Cowling, K. and Mueller, D. 1978: The social costs of monopoly power. *Economic Journal*, 88, 727–48.

Dasgupta, P. E. 1985: The theory of technological competition. In F. Mathewson and J. E. Stiglitz (eds), *New Developments in the Analysis of Market Structure*, London: Macmillan.

Demsetz, H. 1976: Economics as a guide to antitrust regulation. *Journal of Law and Economics*, 19, 371–84.

Dixit, A. K. 1982: Recent developments in oligopoly theory. *American Economic Review*, 72, 12–17.

Easterbrook, F. H. 1984: The limits of antitrust. *Texas Law Review*, 63, 1–40.

Eaton, B. C. and Lipsey, R. 1979: The theory of market preemption: the persistence of excess capacity and monopoly in growing spatial markets. *Economica*, 46, 149–58.

Eaton, B. C. and Lipsey, R. 1981: Capital, commitment and entry equilibrium. *Bell Journal of Economics*, 12, 593–604.

Fox, E. M. 1984: Abuse of a dominant position under the treaty of Rome – a comparison with US law. In *The Annual Proceedings of the Fordham Corporate Law Institute*, Albany: Mathew Bender.

Fudenberg, D., Gilbert, R., Stiglitz, J. and Tirole, J. 1983: Preemption, leapfrogging, and competition in patent races. *European Economic Review*, 22, 3–32.

Fudenberg, D. and Tirole, J. 1983: Learning by doing and market performance. *Bell Journal of Economics*, 14, 522–30.

Fudenberg, D. and Tirole, J. 1984: The fat-cat effect, the puppy-dog ploy, and the lean and hungry look. *American Economic Review*, 74, 361–6.

Fudenberg, D. and Tirole, J. 1985: Predation without reputation. Department of Economics, MIT, unpublished paper.

Gallini, N. T. 1984: Deterrence by market sharing. *American Economic Review*, 74, 931–41.

Gaskins, D. W. Jr 1971: Dynamic limit pricing: optimal pricing under threat of entry. *Journal of Economic Theory*, 3, 306–22.

Gelman, J. R. and Salop, S. C. 1983: Judo economics: capacity limitation and coupon competition. *Bell Journal of Economics*, 14, 315–25.

Geroski, P. and Jacquemin, A. 1984: Dominant firms and their alleged decline. *International Journal of Industrial Organization*, 2, 1–27.

Gilbert, R. and Newbery, D. 1982: Pre-emptive patenting and the persistence of monopoly. *American Economic Review*, 72, 514–26.

Hannah, L. and Kay, J. A. 1977: *Concentration in Modern Industry*. London: Macmillan.

Harris, C. and Vickers, J. 1985: Patent races and the persistence of monopoly. *Journal of Industrial Economics*, 33, 461–81.

Hilke, J. C. and Nelson, P. B. 1984: Noisy advertising and the predation rule in antitrust analysis. *American Economic Review*, 74, 367–71.

Hillman, A. L. 1984: Preemptive rent seeking and the social cost of monopoly power. *International Journal of Industrial Organization*, 2, 277–81.

Hillman, A. L. and Katz, E. 1984: Risk-averse rent seekers and the social cost of monopoly power. *Economic Journal*, 94, 104–10.

Joskow, P. L. and Klevorick, A. K. 1979: A framework for analysing predatory pricing policy. *Yale Law Journal*, 89, 27–37.

Judd, K. L. 1985: Credible spatial preemption. *Rand Journal of Economics*, 16, 153–166.

Kreps, D. and Wilson, R. 1982: Reputation and imperfect information. *Journal of Economic Theory*, 27, 253–79.

Landes, W. M. and Posner, R. A. 1981: Market power in antitrust cases. Harvard Law Review, 94, 937–96.

Lane, W. J., Jr 1980: Product differentiation in a model with endogenous sequential entry. *Bell Journal of Economics*, 11, 237–60.

Leffler, K. 1985: Toward a reasonable rule of reason: comments. *Journal of Law and Economics*, 28, 381–6.

Lewis, T. R. 1983: Preemption, divestiture, and forward contracting in a market dominated by a single firm. *American Economic Review*, 73, 1092–101.

Lieberman, M. K. 1984: The learning curve and pricing in the chemical processing industries. *Rand Journal of Economics*, 15, 213–28.

Mankiw, N. G. and Whinston, M. D. 1985: Free entry and social inefficiency. Harvard Institute of Economic Research, Cambridge, Mass., discussion paper 1125.

Milgrom, P. and Roberts, J. 1982: Predation, reputation, and entry deterrence. *Journal of Economic Theory*, 27, 443–59.

Mueller, D. 1977: The persistence of profits above the norm. *Economica*, 44, 369–80.

Nordhaus, W. D. 1969: *Invention, Growth, and Welfare*. Cambridge, Mass.: MIT Press.

Ordover, J. and Willig, R. D. 1981: An economic definition of predation: pricing and product innovation. *Yale Law Journal*, 91, 8–53.

Overstreet, T. R., Jr 1983: *Resale Price Maintenance: economic theories and empirical evidence*. Washington DC: Federal Trade Commission.

Perry, M. K. 1984: Scale economies, imperfect competition, and public policy. *Journal of Industrial Economics*, 32, 313–30.

Posner, R. A. 1975: The social costs of monopoly and regulation. *Journal of Political Economy*, 83, 807–28.

Posner, R. A. 1976: *Antitrust Law: an economic perspective*. Chicago: University of Chicago Press.

Prescott, E. and Visscher, M. 1977: Sequential location among firms with foresight. *Bell Journal of Economics*, 8, 378–93.

Reinganum, J. 1983: Uncertain innovation and the persistence of monopoly. *American Economic Review*, 73, 741–8.

Roberts, J. 1985: Battles for market share: incomplete information, aggressive strategic pricing, and competitive dynamics. Graduate School of Business, Stanford University, unpublished paper.

Saloner, G. 1985: Predation, mergers and incomplete information. Department of Economics, MIT, working paper 383.

Salop, S. C. 1979: Strategic entry deterrence. *American Economic Review*, 69, 335–8.

Salop, S. C. and Scheffman, D. 1983: Raising rivals' costs. *American Economic Review*, 73, 265–71.

Scharfstein, D. 1984: A policy to prevent rational test-market predation. *Rand Journal of Economics*, 15, 229–43.

Scherer, F. M. 1976: Predatory pricing and the Sherman Act: a comment. *Harvard Law Review*, 89, 868–90.

Scherer, F. M. 1977: *The Economic Effects of Compulsory Patent Licensing*. New York: New York University, Graduate School of Business Administration, Center for the Study of Financial Institutions.

Scherer, F. M. 1980: *Industrial Market Structure and Economic Performance*, 2nd edn. Chicago: Rand-McNally.

Schmalensee, R. 1976: Is more competition necessarily good? *Industrial Organization Review*, 4, 120–1.

Schmalensee, R. 1978: Entry deterrence in the ready-to-eat breakfast cereal industry. *Bell Journal of Economics*, 9, 305–27.

Schmalensee, R. 1979: On the use of economic models in antitrust: the ReaLemon case. *University of Pennsylvania Law Review*, 127, 994–1050.

Schmalensee, R. 1981a: Economies of scale and barriers to entry. *Journal of Political Economy*, 89, 1228–38.

Schmalensee, R. 1981b: Monopolistic two-part pricing arrangements. *Bell Journal of Economics*, 11, 445–66.

Schmalensee, R. 1982a: Antitrust and the new industrial economics. *American Economic Review*, 72, 24–8.

Schmalensee, R. 1982b: Another look at market power. *Harvard Law Review*, 95, 1789–816.

Schmalensee, R. 1982c: Product differentiation advantages of pioneering brands. *American Economic Review*, 72, 349–65.

Schmalensee, R. 1983: Advertising and entry deterrence: an exploratory model. Journal of Political Economy, 91, 636–53.

Schumpeter, J. 1942: *Capitalism, Socialism, and Democracy*. New York: Harper.

Schwartz, M. 1984: Welfare effects of exit-inducing innovations. Economic Policy Office, US Department of Justice, Washington, Discussion paper 84–12.

Spence, A. M. 1977: Entry, capacity, investment and oligopolistic pricing. *Bell Journal of Economics*, 9, 534–44.

Spence, A. M. 1981a: Competition, entry, and antitrust policy. In S. Salop (ed.), *Strategy, Predation, and Antitrust Analysis*. Washington DC: Federal Trade Commission.

Spence, A. M. 1981b: The learning curve and competition. *Bell Journal of Economics*, 12, 49–70.

Stigler, G. J. 1950: Monopoly and oligopoly by merger. *American Economic Review*, 40, 23–34.

Stigler, G. J. 1964: A theory of oligopoly. *Journal of Political Economy*, 72 44–61.

Stigler, G. J. 1965: The dominant firm and the inverted umbrella. *Journal of Law and Economics*, 8, 167–71.

Tullock, G. 1980: Efficient rent-seeking. In J. M. Buchanan, R. D. Tollison and G. Tullock (eds), *Toward a Theory of the Rent-Seeking Society*, Texas A & M University Press, College Station.

US Department of Justice 1984: *Merger Guidelines*. In *Antitrust and Trade Regulation Report*, special supplement S-1-S-16.

Varian, H. 1985: Price discrimination and social welfare. *American Economic Review*, 75, 870–5.

88   RICHARD SCHMALENSEE

von Weizsäcker, C. C. 1980a: *Barriers to Entry: a theoretical treatment.* Berlin: Springer-Verlag.
von Weizsäcker, C. C. 1980b: A welfare analysis of barriers to entry. *Bell Journal of Economics*, 11, 399–420.
Weiss, L. W. and Pascoe, G. 1984: The extent and permanence of market dominance. International Institute of Management, Berlin, IIM/IP discussion paper 84–23.
Williamson, O. E. 1968: Economies as an antitrust defense: the welfare tradeoffs. *American Economic Review*, 58, 18–34.
Williamson, O. E. 1977: Predatory pricing: a strategic and welfare analysis. *Yale Law Journal*, 87, 284–340.
Worcester, D. 1957: Why dominant firms decline. *Journal of Political Economy*, 65, 338–47.

3

Information and Collusion

LOUIS PHLIPS

The topic of information and collusion is both old and brand new. It is old, in the sense that it was discussed at length in the 1950s and 1960s and that precise policy implications were derived and implemented. In Europe, the discussion was couched in terms of 'market transparency' and the impact of improved transparency on the competitive behaviour of oligopolists. In the US, the discussion centred on 'open price systems'. The embarrassing conclusion was that market transparency among competitors does not promote competition but, instead, makes easier a tacit collusion among oligopolists. This was embarrassing since the Arrow–Debreu approach was riding high, so that theoreticians were sticking to the belief that better information is welfare improving *per se* and were splendidly ignoring the conclusions of the debate among antitrust specialists. The latter, on the other hand, ignored welfare economics and did not hesitate to make illegal the information sharing agreements or devices among oligopolists.

Today, we are confronted with what looks like an invasion of the field by game theorists, who – after playing for some time with the concepts of incomplete information and imperfect competition – have come to sharpen their tools to the extent that they now seem capable of deriving policy conclusions which shed new light on the old topic and may even lead to a revision of antitrust policy. Since these conclusions have a strong theoretical foundation, there is some hope that antitrust policy might at last be linked with sound economic theory.

The purpose of this paper is to make a heroic attempt at comparing the two approaches, to see to what extent some of the old wood has to be pruned and some of the new should be given a chance to grow. I shall first try to present the old intuitions in some detail, as they transpire in recent EEC antitrust decisions, and then compare these with possibly conflicting game-theoretic findings.

Old Intuitions

Current EEC antitrust policy is directly inspired by a voluminous literature, mostly of German origin, which is itself influenced by American
writings. A typical and influential representative is Mestmäcker (1952),
who carries the reasoning to the extreme conclusion that all forms of information transmission among oligopolists are to be made illegal. The
opposite view, reflecting ideas that are widespread in industrial circles, is
exposed by Behrens (1963). To be honest, I myself defended a viewpoint
(in 1964) that is close to Mestmäcker's. If, in what follows, I were to
criticize some of the antitrust actions currently taken, that would
admittedly imply a change in beliefs.

The Wood Pulp Decision

The position of the EEC Commission with respect to information transmission among oligopolists can be reconstructed by analysing a number
of decisions taken since 1974.[1] In each case, the basic criterion used is a
situation of *normal competition*, more or less synonymous (I assume)
with the concept of active competition. Before trying to determine what
the Commission considers normal, it may be of some help to take a
closer look at the December 1984 wood pulp decision, in which the Commission's views are expressed in great detail.

   In 1981 six Canadian wood pulp producers, ten American, eleven
Finnish, ten Swedish, one Norwegian, one Portuguese, and one Spanish,
plus the US Pulp, Paper, and Paperboard Association, the Finnish common sales agency and the Swedish Association of Wood Pulp Producers,
were informed that the Commission had found evidence of collusive
behaviour with regard to the prices of their exports to the EEC.

   The main evidence given is the fact that, from 1975 to 1981, these
prices moved in a parallel way. Indeed, these firms were observed to
match competitors' price changes within hours or days. In fact, individual
prices were announced to clients, agencies, or the press (verbally, by
telephone, in writing, or by telex) a few weeks in advance for the next
quarter. All competitors were thus immediately informed of a future

---

[1] See the IFTRA decision of 15 May 1974 (*Official Journal* L 160), the Cobelpa
decision (*OJ* L 242, 21 March 1977), the vegetal parchment decision
(*OJ* L 70, 13 March 1978), the Céruse decision of 12 December 1978 (*OJ* L 21),
the zinc decision of 14 December 1982 (*OJ* L 362), and most recently the wood
pulp decision of 19 December 1984 (*OJ* L 85/1).

price change and were given the opportunity to match it by announcing an identical change. As a result, the announced prices were identical in the north-west of Europe and almost identical in the south of Europe. Transaction prices were most often identical with the announced prices, since very few customers received genuine rebates (as opposed to just the usual payment facilities). All price announcements were in US dollars rather than in the local European currencies.

All addressees, except one American, the Norwegian, the Portuguese, and the Spanish, had to pay (within three months) fines ranging between 50 000 and 500 000 ECU. The fines imposed on the Finnish and Swedish producers were reduced to take account of the fact that they agreed to reduce the 'artificial transparency' of the market by quoting prices in local currencies and to refrain from making announcements on a quarterly basis, from exchanging information about prices or other confidential data, and . . . from colluding.

Normal Competition

A careful reading of the decision suggests that, in the Commission's view, normal competition is characterized by the following ingredients:

Proposition 1 Normal competition implies the freedom, for each individual firm, to change its prices independently.

Anything that affects this freedom is an illegal restriction of competition. This includes price agreements, needless to say, but also any discussion between competitors of their current or future prices *and* of the market conditions that make it possible for a firm to change or not to change its prices.

Proposition 2 Price competition between oligopolists typically takes the form of secret rebates, given for particular transactions, on list prices.

The secrecy of the rebate is the feature that prevents oligopolistic competitors from reacting immediately to a price reduction by one of them and thus makes price competition effective. Without secrecy, the reaction would be immediate and therefore the price reduction would not be granted. In addition, these rebates should be real rebates, not just payment facilities granted to a select group of large customers. (The fact that such rebates imply price discrimination, which is illegal, is not stressed.)

Proposition 3 Normal competition is not compatible with simultaneous moves of transaction prices (and thus of secret rebates) or list prices.

Indeed, if each firm is free to change its prices, simultaneous moves are not to be expected. Each firm will act according to its own individual interest, changing its list price or its transaction price at the optimal time. As a result, if oligopolistic prices display parallel moves, this very fact proves that there is collusion.

Proposition 4 Imperfect information among sellers strengthens the bargaining position of their customers and thus leads to lower transaction prices.

Indeed, it is costly for a firm to check whether a competitor is quoting a low price, as claimed by its customers, so that it will more readily concede a price reduction. When customers are able to play this game simultaneously, average price will go down.

Proposition 5 Perfect information among competitors is not only a necessary condition for collusion but also a sufficient condition, since oligopolists want to collude.

Without market transparency about prices or quantities, colluders cannot enforce a price agreement, i.e. punish the cheater. With market transparency, they will maximize joint profits overtly or tacitly or follow the price leader's moves without delay.

Proposition 6 Multilateral information transmission among oligopolists is therefore *per se* evidence of collusion.

The transmission of information about *current* prices or quantities is a substitute for a formal price agreement since this information is all that is needed for collusion to work.

Proposition 7 Multilateral information transmission about *future* prices is, to an even greater extent, *per se* evidence of collusion.

To discuss or communicate current prices or production rates is bad. To discuss or communicate future prices or production rates is even worse, since the freedom to change in the future is thus also restricted. More or less simultaneous announcements are substitutes for dinner meetings of colluding oligopolists.

Proposition 8 Unilateral information transmission about future prices is also *per se* evidence of collusion, since it could have no other purpose.

Why, indeed, would an individual firm bother to announce a price change publicly (by issuing a press release, circulating a new price list, or sending telexes to customers or agents) if not to make sure that competitors are informed in time to be able to make similar moves?

The Possibility of Non-Cooperative Equilibrium

This enumeration of the informational requirements of active competition is not meant to be exhaustive. It is sufficient, though, to leave one with uneasy feelings.

First, there obviously is no reference to a possible non-cooperative equilibrium. Normal competition is seen as active competition – as implying independent moves by individual firms resulting from bargaining between a particular seller and a particular buyer, and leading to price undercutting.

Secondly, no mention is made of a lower limit at which there would be no possibility of further price decreases. Theoreticians will no doubt emphasize that the lower limit is where price equals marginal cost. But marginal cost is not generally taken as a legal criterion in court discussions or in official decisions by the Commission of the EEC. Admittedly, the idea that a price is above marginal cost and therefore too high may pop up occasionally, but it seems fair to say that Pareto optimality is not the stated objective of current antitrust prolicy.

Thirdly, the implicit assumption seems to be that the only conceivable oligopolistic equilibrium is the collusive one. If prices do not move, there must be a collusive equilibrium. If prices move simultaneously, or almost simultaneously, this must be a move from one collusive equilibrium to another collusive equilibrium. If one firm changes its price, and the others follow immediately or almost immediately, this must be interpreted as a defensive reaction to maintain the agreed market shares. Consequently, competition among oligopolists is possible only through (what game theorists call) cheating. Therefore cheating has to be encouraged by all means. And the best encouragement is to create or maintain imperfect information among competitors.

The time has come to turn to game theory and to introduce the by now trivial idea that an oligopolistic industry can be in equilibrium (so that no firm has any incentive to change its price or production rate) without there being any collusion. There is no co-operation whatsoever, either tacit or explicit, and yet no firm actively tries to increase its market share! There is competition, and yet no firm actively fights its competitors – because it is in no firm's individual interest to engage in active competition! Needless to say, I am referring to a *non-cooperative Nash equilibrium*, which is a set of best replies such that no firm has an incentive to move as long as all other firms stick to their equilibrium positions. These positions may be defined in terms of equilibrium values of production rates, in which case one talks about a Cournot-Nash equilibrium. (Oddly the old, much criticized Cournot equilibrium, if correctly understood, turns out to be a Nash equilibrium with quantity strategies. This, I emphasize, is not a sufficient reason to reject the Nash equilibrium as unrealistic. On the contrary, it should encourage us to throw away the incorrect interpretations of the Cournot equilibrium to which we may have been exposed.) When prices are the strategic variables, one talks about Bertrand-Nash equilibria, in honour of Cournot's critic (who understood Cournot no better than we once did).

The least I hope for is that we all agree that antitrust authorities, lawyers, judges, and experts cannot continue to ignore the concept of a Nash equilibrium, which is at least as much a theoretical possibility as the equality of price and marginal cost. But I am ready to go many steps further, even though I know that much work remains to be done on practical questions such as: how a given industry can be identified as being in a Nash equilibrium; how it gets into such an equilibrium; how it gets out of it; and how it moves from one such equilibrium to another. Progress in this direction will be made only to the extent that the people involved in antitrust cases begin to take the concept seriously.

Even if many of these questions cannot yet be answered in practice, I argue that the present state of the art allows us to go a few steps further. The first thing we can do – and later I shall make an effort in this direction – is to study the properties of a Nash equilibrium and compare these with those of a collusive equilibrium, to see, for example, which types of behaviour or which informational requirements (if any) are typical for the latter and can thus be identified clearly as implying collusion. If both equilibria turn out to have the same informational requirements or to imply the same behaviour, we should doubt that parallel behaviour and information transmission are *per se* evidence of collusion.

The next step is a more difficult one to agree on. I consider active competition as one way to get an industry out of a collusive equilibrium and move it into a Nash equilibrium. I am ready therefore to argue that the Nash equilibrium provides the equilibrium concept that is missing in the propositions listed above, and defines the lower limit to which active competition should reduce industry prices or the upper limit to which active competition should push industry production. Once this limit is reached, no oligopolist has an incentive to break through it. To break through it would be against everybody's interest; perhaps this is what industry circles call 'ruinous competition' (although the same word could designate the collapse of a collusive equilibrium). At any rate, nothing allows us to interpret such terminology as obviously referring to the breakdown of collusion. The words could have their true meaning; now that the concept of a Nash equilibrium exists, and that the possibility of its occurring in the real world must be granted, it seems unfair not to allow for this possibility.

My last step is likely to meet strong opposition. To state it bluntly: to reach a non-cooperative Nash equilibrium is the best that antitrust policy can hope for in oligopolistic markets (which is a far-reaching statement, given that most real-world markets are oligopolistic).

Let me make this statement a bit more precise and insist that, given the multiplicity of possible Nash equilibria, I mean a 'perfect' non-cooperative Nash equilibrium (in quantities or prices, according to the strategies chosen by the industry). Such a perfect Nash equilibrium is part of a two-stage equilibrium[2], in which the other stage implies a market structure that is endogenously determined by the given technology and given tastes. If at a given time, the demand is such and the technology is such that, with free entry, there is room for say only two firms with a given number of products each, and if prices and quantities are at the non-cooperative Nash equilibrium levels, what more can an antitrust authority ask for? Should it call for active competition that would bring prices down to even lower levels? Should it object to the absence of price changes if market conditions are such that no price changes are called for?

Pervasive to the entire argument is the idea that antitrust authorities are *not* social planners. A social planner wants price equal to marginal cost, plus optimal taxes or subsidies. Antitrust authorities want the best possible market structure given technology and tastes, and – given this market structure – as much competition as is compatible with it and with entrepreneurial freedom. But that is precisely, it seems to me, what is described by a perfect non-cooperative Nash equilibrium.

A final warning is in order. In the preceding discussion, 'the' non-cooperative Nash equilibrium has been contrasted with collusion. The time has come to recall that, alas, collusive outcomes may be sustained at a non-cooperative Nash equilibrium, when a game is played repeatedly, so that none of the colluders has an incentive to cheat (as explained in some detail

[2] See Shaked and Sutton (1987).

in Geroski et al., 1985). In particular, one possible collusive outcome that is
directly relevant here and is known as conscious parallelism – the matching
of price changes announced in advance by competitors – can be modelled
as a (perfect) non-cooperative dynamic Nash equilibrium (MacLeod,
1985). It is this type of combination of a collusive outcome with non-
cooperative behaviour that gives a precise meaning to the otherwise vague
concept of tacit collusion.

It should be clear, therefore, that the Nash equilibrium referred to above
is a particular one: it is a perfect non-cooperative *and* non-collusive Nash
equilibrium (whether static or dynamic). To avoid tedious repetition, this
particular equilibrium will be designated in what follows as an NE.

Again, such an NE may be a set of quantity strategies or a set of price
strategies (in this sense, it is not unique either). This should not trouble us
(contrary to a still widespread opinion) since the nature of the product – the
extent of product differentiation and storability – determines which of
these strategies (quantity or price) is relevant.

New Insights

To check whether all this is more than loose speculation, I suggest the
following exercise. Let us consider such an NE, write down propositions
corresponding with the eight propositions above, and describe the relevant
properties of each. I will have reached my objective if the simple juxtaposi-
tion of these gives rise to doubts about the truth of at least one proposition stated above. I must confess I have doubts about several.

Proposition 1'   In an NE, each individual firm is free to change its prices
(or quantities), but it is in the interests of none to do so independently.

Agreements to set or maintain prices are of course by definition incompat-
ible with an NE. But why should non-colluding oligopolists not be allowed
to discuss whether the NE is unchanged, i.e. whether the others think that
the current prices or quantities can be left unchanged, and therefore
whether the market conditions (demand, costs, inventories, and so on)
have changed? To raise or lower one's price makes sense only if all other
competitors do the same, since one firm is in NE only on the condition that
all others are. To act independently is foolish since no firm is independent
of the others.

Proposition 2'   In an NE, there is no room for secret rebates.

Cheating makes sense only if there is collusion. Since there is no collusion
here, there is no need either to prevent cheating or to make secret moves to

prevent competitors from reacting immediately. On the contrary, if one firm moves it expects its competitors to move in the same direction. If they don't it must conclude that it misinterpreted the market situation. Yet nothing prevents the firms involved from giving genuine rebates in the open, i.e. price discrimination is compatible with an NE.

Proposition 3' Successive Nash equilibria are compatible with simultaneous moves of list prices and transaction prices.

Although there are no secret rebates, transaction prices can differ from list prices, for example if a rebate is required in a particular transaction (for a particular location, say, or for a particular delivery date). At any rate, if market conditions change in the same direction for all (aggregate demand increases or falls, or wage rates move up in the same way for all), simultaneous moves are to be expected. If the first to move makes the correct decision, one should expect all competitors to follow within days or hours. If the same firm is repeatedly the first to move, what looks like price leadership develops. Simultaneous moves are not *per se* evidence of collusion.[3]

Proposition 4' An NE requires neither perfect nor complete information.

Analytically, the NE of a game can be found (by game theorists) even if the players do not know each other's profit functions or strategies with certainty (this is a game with incomplete information).[4] The same is true for games in which the history of the game, including today's moves, is not perfectly observable (these are games with imperfect information). Hopefully, real-world oligopolists are able to find their NE in the same circumstances using some rule of thumb such as cost-plus or normal costing. It is doubtful, therefore, that the strengthening of the buyers' bargaining position (emphasized in proposition 4) must lead to a price war.

---

[3] MacLeod (1985, p. 41) arrives at the same conclusion:

> Given that an industry faces a common shock, such as a change in demand or an increase in factor costs, can one distinguish between the static Nash equilibrium . . . and the collusive equilibrium based only on observed price responses? We would say no. . . . In terms of *timing* one would expect all firms to respond at the same time to exogenous shocks, regardless whether collusion is occurring or not. In terms of the size of price changes, again little can be said. . . . Without specific knowledge of the profit functions there would be no systematic differences between the size of price responses at the non-cooperative and collusive equilibria.

[4] See Geroski et al. (1985) and the references given there.

Proposition 5' The implementation of tacit or explicit collusion requires perfect information, since colluders have an incentive to cheat. In addition, however, the difficulties due to incomplete information have to be overcome.

Proposition 5 ignored the fact that potential colluders may not be able to observe each other's preferences (profit functions) and reduced the problem of implementing collusion to the detection and punishment of cheating. Proposition 5' recognizes the importance of perfect information, but insists that, even if information is perfect, collusion does not automatically result. If potential colluders are not able to observe each other's profit functions, they each have private information and must be given an incentive to reveal it correctly (on this see Roberts, 1985). While proposition 5 gives the impression that collusion is easy and therefore ubiquitous, proposition 5' reminds us that collusion is not only difficult to implement, once reached, because of the prisoner's dilemma,[5] but is also difficult to achieve because there are two types of information involved. To be well informed about how competitors are currently behaving is not the same thing as being well informed about the competitors' decision parameters. Market transparency therefore does not guarantee that there is collusion. The presumption that market transparency (among oligopolists) is evidence of collusion should rather be based on the following proposition.

Proposition 6' In an NE, it is not in the oligopolists' interests to share information, but it is in their individual interests to acquire more information.

This proposition is due to Novshek and Sonnenschein (1982) and Clarke (1983). If information sharing leads to perfect information, if perfect information is a necessary ingredient of collusion, *and* if a non-cooperative equilibrium provides no incentive for such information sharing (or even an incentive not to share information, as argued by Clarke), then the current distrust of information sharing agreements can be given a sound theoretical foundation. However, under discussion are schemes that systematically pool all current information available to all colluders, so that information *is* perfect. A case in point, which almost exactly illustrates the model set up by Novshek, Sonnenschein, and Clarke, is the agreement between OPEC and an independent agency that will collect

[5] See Geroski et al. (1985).

complete daily information on oil extraction and shipments by OPEC members.

I wonder whether proposition 6' applies to the transmission of price or quantity data, by individual firms, via press releases, telexes, or letters – or even to meetings where competitors discuss their price or production policies. When a pooling scheme is in operation, such messages or meetings are superfluous. Could not these messages or meetings simply reflect everybody's interest in getting more information – the more so as one cannot presume that more information is all that is needed for collusion to work?

Proposition 7'   Communication about future prices may be a way of getting better information about a new NE.

Suppose industry demand displays seasonal fluctuations, as is the case in the wood pulp industry. Under explicit collusion, the cartel would collectively announce in advance a price schedule covering the entire year. (The announced price changes would be smaller or larger depending on the possibility of building up inventories and depending on whether inventories are built up at the producer or at the customer level.[6]) Perfect intertemporal information (complete certainty) about prices is thus obtained, in the same way as a pooling scheme provides perfect information about current prices, and the freedom to change prices in the future is collectively restricted.

Now, if firms individually announce prices valid for the next quarter only (not the next year) and do so in rapid succession within hours or days, this is a substitute for a meeting. (In an explicit collusive arrangement such signalling would be superfluous.) A price announcement may be a way of implementing conscious parallelism, i.e. collusion. But the message may equally be that a firm thinks the old NE to be changed and wishes the others to confirm or contradict. If firms go to the trouble of announcing future quarterly prices in advance, so that competitors have time to confirm or not, this is therefore not evidence of collusion. And if the same firm is always first there is market dominance – but surely that too is not collusion.

Proposition 8'   Advance notice of price changes may serve all sorts of purposes.

Advance notice of a price increase is a classic device to encourage customers to buy now rather than later; the flow of orders is smoothed

[6] See Phlips and Thisse (1981).

over time so that the cost of carrying inventories is shifted from the seller to the buyer. Advance notice of a price decrease provides an incentive to buy later and smooths the rate of production over time. A better understanding of intertemporal profit maximization and of the economics of inventory building may take away some of the current distrust.

To sum up, we cannot avoid the conclusion that the current antitrust attitude with respect to information acquisition and pooling rests on shaky grounds, to the extent that it considers any communication between oligopolists as evidence of collusion. Careful distinctions have to be drawn. The quest for perfect information on current behaviour has to be distinguished from transmission of information about preferences (i.e. the quest for complete information about profit functions and strategies). Pooling schemes are not synonymous with discussions about current or future prices or quantities; the former are proof of collusion, the latter may occur between non-cooperating competitors. Advance notification cannot be said to be bad as such. And information about prices should not, in principle, be considered more dangerous than information about quantities, since quantity can be a strategic variable as well as price, especially for homogeneous goods.

Are we to conclude that *per se* rules are to be avoided and that we should more carefully weigh the pros and cons in each case? I would hate such a conclusion, not only since it is no conclusion at all, but especially since it leaves business with no indication about what is legal and what is not. We must, somehow, sharpen our economics to the extent that *per se* illegal behaviour can be defined.

Collusive Information Transmission

It is easy to establish a list of explicitly collusive types of behaviour that are illegal. Nobody disputes the fact that signing a cartel agreement is illegal. The question really is which types of behaviour are *tacitly* collusive and therefore also illegal. In the discussion above one such type was identified – a scheme for the systematic pooling of current information with the purpose of creating perfect information – by comparing the incentives for information transmission in an NE with the incentive properties of a collusive outcome. Can we identify other such practices by the same method?

Tying Clauses

Non-systematic transmission of current information – i.e. sporadic transmission from a particular firm to another – by direct or indirect means has been seen to be compatible with the search for a non-cooperative equilibrium in the discussion of proposition 6′. The same must be true for non-systematic acquisition of current information.

An example that comes to mind is a provision that required buyers of Northern Pacific's land to ship timber produced on this land via the Northern Pacific Railway *unless lower rates or better services were available from competing railway lines.* As argued by Cummings and Ruhter (1979), the main purpose of such clauses is not to tie the shipping with the purchase of land, but to compel buyers to disclose the lower rate or better service offered by competing carriers (the tying arrangement simply provided protection against non-reporting). Such contracts imply no obligation for the seller to meet lower prices, so that there is no automatic deterrence of cheating (in contrast with 'meet competition' clauses). As such they are competitive rather than collusive.

Another classic example is the International Salt case. Following Peterman (1979), the tying clause used by the International Salt Company can be interpreted as a device to ensure good reporting by the lessees (of a machine that dissolves rock salt) of the competitor's prices of salt, since lessees were free to buy on the open market whenever International Salt failed to meet these prices.

Meet Competition Clauses

A meet competition clause entitles a buyer who finds another seller offering a lower price to this same lower price. If the clause also contains a release option, so that the buyer can choose to be released of this contractual obligation, I am ready to argue that this is again an innocent information acquisition device; it is only by informing his original supplier that the buyer can escape from his obligation to purchase. But he *can* escape from this obligation. And this freedom gives the buyer an incentive to enter long-term arrangements which he might otherwise be hesitant to sign.

Deletion of the release option, however, transforms the clause into a powerful deterrent to cheating. Now the competitors know that this firm will retaliate to any detected price reduction and that customers will report any price reduction immediately to it. The deterrence effect is maximized. And since deterrence is a problem only in a collusive arrangement, the clause (without release) must be collusive.

Salop (1985) has illustrated the deterrence effect with respect to the prisoner's dilemma in a game with two players (Ethyl and Du Pont, say). First, the achievement of a collusive equilibrium is facilitated, since one firm can raise its price to the collusive level without losing any sales to a lower-priced rival in the transition period during which the rival sticks to the lower price. In addition, the rival is encouraged not to delay a matching price increase, since the transitional gains that could result from his lower price are eliminated by the clause. Secondly, once the collusive outcome is reached, it is stabilized. Indeed, with no-release meeting competition clauses on both sides, it becomes impossible for one player to undercut the other; the only possibilities are to stick to the collusive equilibrium or to shift to an NE. The threat of such a shift is very credible and therefore effective. It can be reinforced by a 'most favoured nation' clause.

Most Favoured Nation (MFN) Clauses

An MFN clause guarantees the buyer any discount offered to another buyer by the (same) seller under the terms of the contract. The clause can be retroactive or contemporaneous.

Consider *retroactive* MFN clauses first. These prevent price reductions if the market deteriorates, since later price reductions must be applied to some past sales. Their objective is thus to make prices stickier over time, and to keep them at the collusive level. Salop (1985, table 3) again illustrates the mechanism with respect to the prisoner's dilemma by showing that, with a retroactive MFN clause, gains from retaliating are relatively smaller than in the absence of such clauses. Adjustments to changing market conditions (typical for non-collusive Nash equilibria) are prevented. In particular, a shift to the non-collusive NE is made relatively more unprofitable. The effect of a meeting competition clause is thus reinforced.

A *contemporaneous* MFN clause penalizes and deters only price cuts that are restricted to a limited number of customers. Retaliation with a general price reduction is not penalized.

If nobody offers an MFN, selective discounts may develop and imperfect information may destabilize a collusive equilibrium. If one firm unilaterally institutes a contemporaneous MFN, it commits itself to retaliating only with a general price cut to all its customers (starting a price war, in fact). Its rivals will conclude that, since a general price cut is costly and easily detected, there will be no retaliation if they approach only a limited number of customers of the firm that instituted the MFN. Collusion is thus reinforced. If all competitors institute an MFN, selective discounts will not be matched (since this would imply a general price cut) if they are restricted to a limited number of the rivals' customers. On the one hand, price undercutting is restricted in scope. On the other hand, the threat of a shift to a non-cooperative NE is made more credible. Finally, if an MFN clause is combined with a meeting competition clause, the threat is reinforced and the need to actually carry it out may be reduced (Salop, 1985).

Conclusion

Recent EEC antitrust policy tends to consider any information transmission among oligopolists as proof of tacit collusion. This paper argues that such policy lacks sound theoretical foundations and suggests an analysis in terms of the informational requirements of a non-cooperative Nash equilibrium versus those of a collusive equilibrium. The necessity and possibility of establishing a restrictive list of informational practices that are collusive *per se* is also emphasized, as is the compatibility of information transmission and non-collusive behaviour.

References

Behrens, F.-S. 1963: *Marktinformation und Wettbewerb*. Cologne: Carl Heymans.

Clarke, R. N. 1983: Collusion and the incentives for information sharing. *Bell Journal of Economics*, 14, 383–94.

Cummings, F. J. and Ruther, W. E. 1979: The *Northern Pacific* case. *Journal of Law and Economics*, 22, 329–50.

Geroski, P., Phlips, L. and Ulph, A. 1985: Oligopoly, competition and welfare: some recent developments. *Journal of Industrial Economics*, symposium on oligopoly, competition and welfare, 33, 369–86.

MacLeod, W. B. 1985: A theory of conscious parallelism. *European Economic Review*, 27, 25–44.

Mestmäcker, E.-J. 1952: Verbandsstatistiken als Mittel zur Beschränkung und Förderung des Wettbewerbs in den Vereinigten Staaten und Deutschland. Frankfurt-on-Main, dissertation.

Novshek, A. and Sonnenschein, H. 1982: Fulfilled expectations: Cournot duopoly with information acquisition and release. *Bell Journal of Economics*, 13, 214–18.

Peterman, J. L. 1979: The *International Salt* case. *Journal of Law and Economics*, 22, 351–64.

Phlips, L. 1964: Markttransparenz in Theorie und Wirklichkeit. *Wirtschaft und Wettbewerb*, 14, 205–11.

Phlips, L. and Thisse, J.-F. 1981: Pricing, distribution and the supply of storage. *European Economic Review*, 15, 225–43.

Roberts, K. 1985: Cartel behaviour and adverse selection. *Journal of Industrial Economics*, symposium on oligopoly, competition and welfare, 33, 401–13.

Salop, S.C. 1985: Practices that (credibly) facilitate oligopoly coordination. In F. Mathewson and J. E. Stiglitz (eds), *New Developments in the Analysis of Market Structure*, London: Macmillan.

Shaked, A. and Sutton, J. 1987: Product differentiation and industrial structure. *Journal of Industrial Economics*, 1987.

4

The Interaction of Market Structure and Conduct

GEORGE A. HAY

Introduction

Competition policy in the US has undergone considerable change in recent years. To the casual observer, this is merely a political phenomenon, attributable to the *laissez-faire* economic philosophy of the present administration, and subject to reversal should the Democrats regain power. But for many who are professionally involved in competition policy, the change is seen not as a transient phenomenon but as a longer-term trend reflecting the gradually increasing influence of economics and economists since the early 1970s.[1]

[1] Within the Antitrust Division, the influence of economists has been reflected in two significant changes in its organizational structure. In 1973, the Economic Policy Office was established and a serious (and successful) effort was begun to recruit a large number of Ph.D. economists with the best academic credentials. Throughout the next 12 years, the number of such economists grew steadily even as the number of attorneys in the Division was shrinking by one-third. In 1985, the chief economist was elevated to the position of Deputy Assistant Attorney-General with explicit recognition of the importance of economists in the decision-making process of the Antitrust Division. At the Federal Trade Commission, two of the five commissioners in office at the beginning of 1985 were economists.

On the academic front, there has been a large increase in the number of economists who identify themselves as specialists in industrial organization (the American label comparable with industrial economics in the UK.). There has been a qualitative shift as well, with the mathematical content of much of the literature becoming comparable with other branches of economics. The influence of academics can be seen in the frequency with which law review articles relating to antitrust policy are written by economists or at least contain substantial amounts of economic analysis, and in the growing tendency to have economists participate in the teaching of antitrust law at the best American schools. Economists appear regularly on the antitrust programmes of the American Bar

There are several ways in which an economist might describe or characterize the nature of the change in competition policy. My particular interest in this paper is on the role of market structure in the implementation of competition policy and, in particular, on the use of structure in determining the legality or illegality of a firm's conduct.

The policy orientation of the paper is important, since where the inquiry is essentially academic – seeking to understand and evaluate how industries perform – an assessment of market structure and a detailed analysis of firms' conduct will each be important elements in the study, with no need to compare the relative weights given to each element. But competition policy enforcement and academic research are not the same thing, and there may be legitimate reasons for policy-makers to ignore structure where academics might regard it as relevant, or let policy be determined solely by structure where economists would regard structure as merely a part of the relevant data set.

By way of example, consider the antitrust attitude towards simple, horizontal price-fixing. Certainly in the US, and as a practical matter in the UK and the EEC, price-fixing is unlawful regardless of market structure and the collective market power of the would-be price-fixers. Put differently, it is no defence to a charge of price-fixing to assert that the firms involved have no market power.[2]

In contrast, in cases under US law involving horizontal mergers, market structure is not only relevant but until quite recently was the *only*

Association and other continuing legal education programmes, and every major law firm with a serious antitrust practice has a working relationship with one or more economists. One Washington DC law firm even has a subsidiary economic consulting firm.

[2] In some of the early price-fixing cases to come before the US Supreme Court after the passage of the Sherman Act, defendants attempted (unsuccessfully) to show that the Sherman Act did not apply where the firms did not have the power to raise prices to an unreasonable level. The irrelevance of market power in such circumstances was made absolutely clear in *United States* v. *Socony-Vacuum Oil Co.*, 310 US 150 (1940).

The policy arguments for a blanket rule of *per se* illegality for price-fixing are twofold. First, if firms attempt to fix prices they must assume, despite concentration statistics, that they have some collective power over price, since otherwise they would have no reason to engage in the activity. Courts should defer to this assumption, notwithstanding the statistical or other evidence suggesting a lack of power. Secondly, since there is no possible social gain from price-fixing, there is no harm in deterring even those would-be cartels that have no chance of success. Of course, the Department of Justice can exercise prosecutorial discretion not to attack truly impotent cartels.

relevant factor. Where concentration is low (and would not be unduly raised by the combination) mergers have been presumed lawful, and where concentration is high (and would be increased non-trivially by the merger) almost no arguments could be mounted to save the merger from successful challenge.[3] For example, a claim that entry barriers were low or that a merger would produce efficiency gains would not have had much likelihood of success under US case law.[4]

Each of these examples involves issues of collective market power. My interest in this paper is primarily on the implementation of competition policy toward individual firms, but the kinds of questions I ask are similar to those in the examples.[5] Specifically, I am interested in whether the conduct of firms with market power should be evaluated differently from that of firms without such power, and if so, how the evaluation would differ. Can conduct which is regarded as unobjectionable if carried out by firms without market power become the basis for a violation of the antitrust laws when market power is present? Can conduct which is at least arguably objectionable if carried out by firms with market power be disregarded entirely where firms do not possess power?

The analysis is primarily historical. I identify three different phases or modes of antitrust policy towards individual firms and try to show that US policy, having operated in the first mode for much of the period 1945–75, passed through a second mode during 1975–85, and seems about to enter a third. However, while the analysis is historical, it is presented in the belief that there are important lessons to be learned, especially by policy-makers in other jurisdictions such as the UK and the

---

[3] The one long-standing exception is the 'failing company' doctrine. If the acquired firm can show that, but for the merger, it would go out of business and that there are no alternative purchasers that pose less of a competitive problem, the merger will be permitted under US case law despite high market shares.

[4] The 1984 Justice Department Merger Guidelines signal a retreat from the practice of focusing only on concentration. The Guidelines indicate that, where entry barriers are low, mergers will not be challenged regardless of concentration levels, and that claims of efficiencies arising from a proposed merger will be given serious consideration. The Guidelines, it should be noted, reflect merely the enforcement policy of the Justice Department, and are in no way binding on courts that may decide cases where a private plaintiff (typically a firm resisting a hostile takeover attempt) has challenged the merger. However, the Guidelines may be influential on the way courts address merger questions.

[5] I include vertical restraints in the scope of my analysis. Even though such restraints often involve an agreement between two firms, the firms are not competitors and there is normally no issue of collective market power.

EEC who, not having suffered the full range of experimentation that has occurred in the US, may benefit from an evaluation of that experience.

The First Mode of Antitrust Enforcement, 1945–75

At the risk of oversimplification, one can identify three different modes of antitrust policy towards individual firms. The first mode was characterized by great distrust and hostility toward many forms of conduct, without regard to market power.[6] As a consequence, while most activity by firms with small market shares was not attacked, this was not due to confidence that such firms always behaved competitively (or even competently), or to a belief that anticompetitive conduct would be weeded out in the process of interfirm competition. The apparent passivity was due rather to the lack of a statutory basis for challenging such behaviour under the antitrust laws.

As evidence of the underlying hostility, for those pockets of behaviour where a special statutory basis for challenging the conduct existed or where the plaintiff could establish some kind of agreement, small firms were attacked with vigour. Tie-ins, for example, were regarded as virtually illegal *per se*, subject to a fairly modest requirement that the tying product had some degree of 'uniqueness'. (Not infrequently, the fact that the 'victim' accepted the tie was accepted as evidence that such uniqueness must exist.[7]) The same prosecutorial vigour was applied to vertical price-fixing (resale price maintenance), some other vertical arrangements in which the manufacturer restricted competition among its dealers (e.g. customer or territorial allocations), and, to a lesser extent, long-term contractual relationships between buyer and seller such as exclusive purchasing requirements. Moreover, especially with the rapid growth of private antitrust action in the late 1960s and early 1970s, there was a marked tendency to define markets narrowly so as to bring

[6] Frank Easterbrook attributes to Donald Turner the phrase 'the inhospitality tradition of antitrust', in which judges view each business practice with suspicion that firms are using it to harm consumers. See Easterbrook (1984b, p. 4).

[7] Often the only 'uniqueness' present was the especially favourable terms available to consumers willing to take the entire package. See *United States Steel Corp.* v. *Fortner Enterprises, Inc.* (Fortner II), 429 US 610 (1977), where US Steel offered favourable finance terms to customers who purchased certain prefabricated structures from US Steel. It took the Court two tries (spanning eight years) before it was able to conclude that US Steel did not have market power in the market for loans.

more of the behaviour of even relatively small firms within the ambit of antitrust enforcement.

Whatever legal restraints operated on firms without any demonstrable market power were of course applied to firms with market power. But for firms whose degree of market power was sufficient to be characterized as monopoly power, the behavioural restraints were much broader. Indeed, virtually any action taken by a large firm to retain or increase its share was liable to be characterized as 'exclusionary' and condemned as an act of monopolization. Courts would not acknowledge explicitly that monopoly power was illegal *per se*, but their actions suggested otherwise. The one activity expressly permitted was to charge very high prices (an interesting contrast to the UK policy), although since 'excessive' profits could be used as proof of monopoly power, the risk was amplified that plaintiffs would find some other kind of conduct that could be labelled exclusionary and, because of the market power, an act of monopoly. The famous cases involving Alcoa and United Shoe Machinery illustrate this kind of thinking, in which activities that would be totally free from opprobrium if undertaken by small firms are characterized as exclusionary and illegal when they help large firms to maintain their market positions.

Over the years there was a gradual build-up of economic criticism of this first mode of antitrust enforcement. For several reasons, however, the response by policy-makers and courts was slow. First, during the period when most significant monopoly cases and other cases involving individual firms were prosecuted by the Justice Department, prosecutorial discretion could be used to avoid the most obvious situations of attacking truly meritorious conduct. Secondly, those firms which were attacked were seen as having significant monopoly power which required dissipation, and it seemed not a critical fault that the specific reason given for attacking the firms' conduct did not fully meet with economists' approval.

This pattern began to change with the increased use of antitrust action by private plaintiffs in the late 1960s and early 1970s.[8] As suggested earlier, markets in monopolization cases were often defined quite narrowly in private cases, so that many firms without any semblance of what had historically been viewed as real monopoly power found themselves charged

[8] In 1941–50 the average number of private antitrust cases filed each year was 93; in 1951–60 the average was 221; and in 1971–80 the average was 1384. An abundance of data about private antitrust cases and an analysis of some of the data were presented at a recent two-day conference organized by Georgetown University Law School. The papers from the conference will shortly be published in a conference volume.

with monopolization. The courts were swamped with cases, often against relatively small firms, and alleging as anticompetitive much conduct which to the casual observer (and increasingly to the courts) hardly seemed offensive to allocative efficiency or against consumer interests. The fact that many of the cases involved IBM, a firm widely perceived to be among America's most progressive and well-run corporations, made the problem seem even more in need of attention.[9]

The Second Mode of Enforcement, 1975–85

The catalyst for the movement to the second mode of enforcement was the paper by Areeda and Turner (1975) on predatory pricing. As suggested earlier, in the first mode the focus of analysis was on whether the conduct of a dominant firm had an exclusionary effect on rivals, and since low prices are likely to be particularly effective in discouraging or eliminating rivals, it was common to attack low prices as exclusionary and therefore anticompetitive. Areeda and Turner expressed dissatisfaction with this way of analysing pricing, arguing that as long as a firm's price exceeds incremental costs, low prices improve allocative efficiency in the short run; even over a longer period, a rule allowing price reductions as long as price covers incremental costs should discourage or eliminate only less efficient firms, thereby again serving allocative efficiency.

While many economists had expressed these ideas in the past, there had been no apparent impact on the courts. Whether because of the prestige of the authors (Turner had previously been Assistant Attorney-General for antitrust enforcement and Areeda was one of the most prominent antitrust legal scholars in the country), the fact that they were not associated with the University of Chicago (from which attacks on antitrust policy seemed to flow like water from a tap), the prestige of the medium (*Harvard Law Review*), the clarity of the writing (plain English, no equations, and only a few diagrams), or just because it was an idea whose time had come, the ideas took hold. With some variations and modifications, the Areeda–Turner mode of analysis was rapidly adopted by the US courts.[10]

[9] Fisher et al. (1983) provide an animated critique of the claims made against IBM from the perspective of having been IBM's front-line team of economic experts.

[10] For one of many excellent studies of the adoption of the Areeda–Turner model by the courts, see Hurwitz and Kovacic (1982).

As a result, the focus now is on the specific acts of large firms, to determine whether they are anticompetitive in addition to being exclusionary. For strict adherents to the Areeda–Turner rule, this means that behaviour must have short-run misallocative effects to be condemned (e.g. prices below incremental costs). A less drastic and more widely adopted accommodation dictates that where the behaviour is not obviously misallocative in the short run, a clear showing is required that the behaviour is almost certain to so alter the structure of the industry in the direction of single-firm monopoly that the long-run consequences are both serious and imminent. Thus, for example, prices above incremental costs are still subject to challenge, but typically only where they are below average total costs (suggesting that the victim may not be less efficient in the long run), where the number of current competitors to the dominant firm is small and likely to be reduced significantly by the dominant firm's pricing conduct, and where barriers to new entry are high.

What makes the rapid adoption of the Areeda–Turner rule and its variants particularly interesting is that, while the process was occurring, there was a parallel development in the economics literature consisting of numerous papers showing circumstances in which dominant firms can act anticompetitively without pricing below incremental costs, suggesting that the Areeda–Turner test is potentially underinclusive, i.e. some genuine predators will escape condemnation.[11] It is worth noting, however, that the fact that a rule is underinclusive in theory (or even that it will from time to time be underinclusive in actual operation) does not necessarily render the rule a bad policy instrument. This reflects the important difference between economic analysis and policy rules. The key question is how often, in fact, the rule will fail to catch genuine predation, and how serious the consequences of that predation will be.[12] Economists, in their perversity, are capable of constructing all sorts of imaginative scenarios in which firms behave anticompetitively without violating the test, but rarely are they prepared to suggest that such cases will occur with enough frequency to warrant concern.

Moreover, even those economists who, on theoretical grounds, criticize the rule as underinclusive, generally applaud the key philosophical adjustment towards focusing on firms' conduct, and not routinely labelling a firm's actions as anticompetitive merely because

[11] For a survey of this literature, and a discussion of the relevance of the lack of academic consensus, see Brodley and Hay (1981).

[12] For a more detailed discussion of the way to determine an optimal rule, see Joskow and Klevorick (1979).

some individual competitors lose market share. It is also important to be aware that no rule is so airtight as not to admit exceptions, and even were a strict version of the Areeda–Turner test to become 'the law', judges would not be prevented from circumventing the rule in the most egregious cases. Hence, while the economic literature on predatory behaviour continues to expand and the US Supreme Court has yet to consider the validity of the Areeda–Turner rule or any of its variants, there seems little reason to expect a fundamental reversal of this second mode of antitrust analysis.[13]

The Difference between the First and Second Modes: The Case of Michelin

For European readers, an interesting way of illustrating the difference between the first and second enforcement modes is by reference to the European Commission's recent case involving the pricing practices of Michelin, the largest producer of replacement tyres for cars, trucks, and buses.[14] The allegations centred on Michelin's discounts to its dealers. Various aspects of the discount policy were analysed, but the main issue was Michelin's practice of basing annual bonuses to its dealers on the increment of sales over a 'target' based on the previous year's sales.

The Commission's decision (which was upheld in all relevant aspects by the European Court) characterized the bonus scheme as a form of loyalty rebate and complained that the scheme 'restricts dealers' freedom of choice' and is 'aimed at tying the dealers closely to [Michelin] thus making it difficult for other producers to gain a foothold in the market'. The bonuses 'are set and calculated in such a way that in advance [Michelin] gains a hold on the dealer in the efforts he makes to promote Michelin tyres, clearly detrimental to the efforts he puts in for other makes'. Michelin 'is able through the discount system to ensure that it obtains a maximum percentage . . . of the purchases made by dealers'. In the opinion of the Commission such a scheme, when undertaken by a

[13] While the Court has not yet addressed the predatory pricing issue, a recent monopolization case involving a refusal to deal suggests that the Court rejects the notion that anything a firm does to increase market share is exclusionary and therefore anticompetitive, and is prepared to condemn behaviour by large firms only where it is independently misallocative. See *Aspen Skiing Corp.* v. *Aspen Highland Skiing Corp.*, 105 S.Ct. 2847 (1985).

[14] *Nederlandsche Banden-Industrie Michelin* v. *EC Commission* (1985).

firm in a dominant position, constitutes an abuse of that position within the meaning of article 86.

From the rhetoric it sounds very much as though the Commission is operating in the first mode of enforcement, and that Michelin's policy is criticized primarily because it is so effective in maintaining Michelin's market share. Yet it may be possible, without much additional analysis, to show that Michelin's pricing policy is misallocative in the short run and therefore subject to attack even under the second mode. While the Commission's rhetoric speaks of a 'coercion' on the dealers to meet the sales target (by denying them a percentage bonus of all previous sales if they do not), the coercion is nothing more than an extremely large reward for the increment of sales needed to meet the quota.

As a result, Michelin's effective net revenue from the block of purchases that take the dealer over his sales target may be quite low, since when the target is achieved a discount is applied retroactively to earlier purchases. Without more data one cannot be sure, but it is entirely possible that Michelin's effective revenue on this incremental block of sales is below manufacturing costs. If so, these sales may be more than is warranted by allocative efficiency and Michelin's conduct could be attacked under the Areeda–Turner rule.[15]

Predatory Discrimination across Geographic Markets

Another illustration of the difference between the two modes of analysis is provided by Utton's (1979, 1985) discussion of some earlier inquiries by the UK Monopolies and Mergers Commission into the pricing practices of certain dominant firms. Utton makes a convincing case that on several occasions some of the firms under investigation cut prices in order to eliminate a rival competitor. Typically, this was accomplished by a localized price cut in a limited geographic area where rivals had appeared, and the discrimination was effective in maintaining high prices elsewhere (where no serious competition existed). There is no evidence that prices in the 'competitive' markets were below the predator's incremental costs.

---

[15] The analysis is complicated because one would wish to calculate the effective revenue not on a single unit of sales (e.g. the unit that put the dealer over the quota) but on a larger block reflecting the overall impact on the incentive of the dealer to make additional sales. For example, one might examine the block of sales that is the difference between the previous year's sales and the current year's quota. The appropriate block on which to base the calculation will depend on the precise nature of the bonus system.

In the absence of evidence of below-cost pricing, the behaviour would not violate the Areeda–Turner proposed test for predation. This seems unsatisfactory, since it is apparent (in Utton's view) that the intent (and effect) of the pricing was to eliminate competition. On further reflection, however, the dilemma is clear. Where a dominant firm can successfully segregate markets, and discriminate in price so that prices are reduced only in the competitive market, a necessary element in the 'predation' story is missing. Unless prices in the competitive market are below the dominant firm's incremental costs, there is no element of temporary sacrifice in profits. The additional business in the segregated market is profitable at any price above incremental cost. It would be rational for the dominant firm to attempt to capture that business – or any part of it – without regard to whether doing so will lead to the permanent demise of a pesky rival. In short, the pricing behaviour does not misallocate resources in the short run, and would not be condemned in the hard-core version of the second mode of enforcement.

It would still be possible to argue, in the less rigid version of the second mode, that barriers to entry were high and that the victims of the price cut were the only source of competition, such that after their demise the predator would be truly dominant. US courts would also be likely to insist on the evidence of specific intent, i.e. that the price cuts were specifically aimed at eliminating the victim so as to be free of competitive pressure. Even with all this, however, in the absence of some objective standard of anticompetitive pricing (e.g. prices below average total costs) US courts would be reluctant to condemn the behaviour.

The Third Mode of Enforcement, 1985 onwards

The third mode of enforcement shifts the focus from conduct back to structure, but in such a way that it is really an extension of the second mode rather than inconsistent with it. Dominant firm behaviour is still analysed with a view to finding something specifically objectionable rather than attacking any kind of behaviour which tends to retain or increase market share. The novelty of the third mode is in the method of analysing the conduct of non-dominant firms. With certain limited exceptions, the operating principle is to exempt conduct by firms without market power from antitrust scrutiny altogether. This goes well beyond whatever limits are imposed by the statutory scheme since, as indicated earlier, there are ample statutory grounds for examining many kinds of conduct by firms with only modest market shares.

The intellectual foundation for this mode of enforcement is contained in a series of articles by Frank Easterbrook (1984a, 1984b), which in turn were inspired by the earlier writing of Robert Bork (1978). The notion is that modern business is extremely complicated, and firms choose to compete in many ways, some of which may look unusual and even suspicious to the casual observer. Policy-makers, courts, and even 'expert' bodies are not competent to analyse such behaviour correctly with any consistency, and will often leap (incorrectly) to the conclusion that what is new and unusual is also suspicious and probably anticompetitive. As indicated earlier, Easterbrook refers to this as the 'hostility tradition' of antitrust policy.[16]

Such mistaken enforcement is unfortunate and unnecessary, according to Easterbrook, since there is no need for policy-makers to intervene in the conduct of firms without market power in the absence of indications of horizontal agreement. The basic motivation of firms without market power is to please consumers, since only in that way will they succeed in the competitive struggle. Hence there should be a presumption that conduct by such firms, however curious, is in fact efficient and a sensible adaptation to the business environment. But even if it is not, there is no cause for alarm (or intervention). Inefficient behaviour will be weeded out in the competitive struggle, as firms that displease consumers lose out to those that provide the most satisfaction. The process, moreover, will not be appreciably slower and will be certainly more accurate in Easterbrook's view than if policy-makers attempted to impose their views of what is socially optimal.

An Application of the Third Mode: the Vertical Restraint Guidelines

The clearest manifestation of these views in competition policy is the recent Department of Justice Vertical Restraint Guidelines. Vertical restraints are conditions imposed by a manufacturer on its wholesale or retail dealer such as exclusive dealing, territorial or customer restraints, and resale price maintenance.[17] The effect of many vertical restraints, such as territorial allocation or resale price maintenance, is to eliminate intrabrand competition, i.e. competition among dealers of the same

[16] See footnote 6 above.

[17] Other restraints such as tie-ins are regarded by economists as analytically equivalent to vertical restraints. Tie-ins are covered in a separate section of the Guidelines.

manufacturer at the wholesale or retail level. (In territorial allocation, the manufacturer assigns each dealer an exclusive territory. No other dealer is permitted to sell to customers in the chosen dealer's territory, and the chosen dealer is forbidden to sell outside its assigned territory.)

American antitrust policy, and to a lesser extent UK competition policy, has long been hostile to vertical restraints. The primary basis for the hostility is from analogy with a horizontal cartel among the dealers themselves. Such a cartel would normally be regarded as anticompetitive and illegal in both the US and the UK. Hence, according to the analogy, the identical restraint on competition among dealers, even though imposed vertically, has the same economic impact and ought to receive the same legal treatment.[18]

Over the past 20 years, the level of hostility to vertical restraints has been diminishing, largely in response to the explanation by economists of why the analogy with horizontal agreements is inappropriate and how the vertical restraints can actually improve competition among products of different manufacturers.[19] The most recent Supreme Court case[20] to deal directly with the merits of vertical restraints suggested a broad 'rule-of-reason' inquiry into the actual competitive impact of any given vertical (non-price) restraint, without however providing any instructions on how the inquiry was to be performed. (To compound the confusion, the court said it would continue to apply the rule of *per se* illegality to vertical price restraints, thereby causing much subsequent litigation to get bound up in the characterization of a restraint as price or non-price. The general trend, however, has been one of increased freedom for manufacturers to utilize non-price restraints.)

The Justice Guidelines would carry the liberalization even further and would, if adopted by the courts,[21] virtually terminate all litigation

---

[18] Another basis for judicial hostility, especially in the US was the long-standing common law condemnation of restraints on alienation. In the Sylvania case *Continental TV Inc.* v. *GTE Sylvania, Inc.*, 433 US 36 (1979), the Court expressed some doubts about whether the common law condemnation was quite so universal as prior decisions of the Court had suggested.

[19] The classic article is that by Telser (1960). Easterbrook (1984a) contains a similar, but updated, explanation.

[20] This is the Sylvania case. See footnote 18 above.

[21] As with the Merger Guidelines, the Vertical Restraint Guidelines merely reflect the Department's enforcement intentions, and are not binding on the courts. Given that most vertical restraints cases arise in private litigation, however, it is clear that the primary goal of the Guidelines is to educate and influence the courts.

involving vertical non-price restraints.[22] The Guidelines operate so as to screen out without elaborate economic analysis those situations in which vertical restrains are likely to be primarily efficiency creating. Detailed analysis is left only for those restraints that fail to pass this initial screen, and even that analysis is largely confined to examining various observable structural characteristics of the industry.

To perform the screen, the Guidelines define two concepts. The first, called the Vertical Restraints Index (VRI), is analogous to the Herfindahl-Hirschman index (HHI) used in the Merger Guidelines. It is calculated by squaring the market share of each firm in the market which is a party to a contract or other arrangement that contains the vertical restraint, and then summing the values obtained for firms at the same level of operations (i.e. supplier or dealer). For example, if three or four manufacturers, each with a 25 per cent market share, employ a restraint, the VRI $= 25^2 + 25^2 + 25^2 = 1875$. The maximum value that the VRI can take is therefore $100^2 = 10\,000$.

The second concept, called the coverage ratio, is the percentage of each market involved in a restraint. For example, if ten suppliers, each with 5 per cent market shares, employ a restraint, the coverage ratio is 50 per cent. Hence the VRI could be low (because the industry is not highly concentrated) while, at the same time, the coverage ratio is high (since virtually all firms employ the restraint).

Using these two concepts, the screen operates as follows. The use of a vertical restraint will not be challenged if

1 the firm employing the restraint has a market share of 10 per cent or less; or
2 the VRI is under 1200 and the coverage ratio is below 60 per cent in the same market (which can be either the supplier or dealer market); or
3 the VRI is under 1200 in both relevant markets; or
4 the coverage ratio is less than 60 per cent in both markets.

---

[22] The discussion in the text that follows is extracted from Hay (1985). It should be noted that the Guidelines apply only to non-price vertical restraints. In early public statements, the Justice Department had made clear its view that price and non-price vertical restraints were essentially equivalent from an economics perspective and ought to receive identical legal treatment. Congressional reaction to such pronouncements was sufficiently threatening for the Justice Department to no longer openly advocate changing the rule of *per se* illegality for price restraints.

The first test simply provides a safe harbour for small firms on the theory that they are unlikely to be prominent in any cartel or in any effort to facilitate a cartel. The remaining tests are based on the assumption that the restraints are unlikely to facilitate collusion (or to have an exclusionary impact) unless the relevant markets are highly concentrated and the practice is widely used. For situations where the restraints are not immunized with this structural screen, the Guidelines suggest a further examination, focusing primarily on ease of entry and other factors that would render collusion more or less likely, but including other evidence that may shed light on the likely net competitive impact of the restraints. A similar screening process is applied to tie-ins with the effect of providing immunity for firms with less than 30 per cent market share.

It is also important to note that, while the Guidelines speak in terms of market share, the spirit of the exercise involves market power rather than merely market shares, and it may be open to a firm to argue that despite a historical level of sales that yields a high share of some line of business, that share is not representative of market power. Indeed, even under the explicit language of the Guidelines, the methodology for establishing market shares, which is identical to that employed in the Merger Guidelines, is not simply by reference to past sales, but looks to a variety of factors (like the potential for imports or supply substitutability) that might affect future sales.[23]

For the purposes of this paper, the significant aspect of the Guidelines is to shift the focus from conduct back to structure, since if a firm can establish limited market power at the first stage, it escapes scrutiny on conduct altogether. In that respect, there are at least superficial similarities between the third mode of enforcement under US enforcement policy and the statutory scheme in the UK and the EEC. Reference to the UK Monopolies and Mergers Commission (MMC) under the Fair Trading Act requires a 25 per cent market share, and article 86 of the EEC rules involve abuse of a dominant position. However, the appearances of similarity belie the substance.

As far as the UK is concerned, the 1980 Competition Act permits reference either under a market share criterion or under a threshold applied to annual turnover. The latter is low enough that, in industries of any significance, firms can satisfy the threshold without having market shares that approach those usually associated with a significant individual

---

[23] For a discussion of the Merger Guidelines' methodology for estimating market shares, see Hay and Reynolds (1985).

market power. In addition, even under the Fair Trading Act and the 25 per cent threshold, the standards for market definition (with respect to which shares are measured) seem not to be particularly rigorous and there seems to be little opportunity to challenge (at the reference stage) a narrow market definition.[24]

For the EEC, some of the kinds of activities that are subject to the third mode of enforcement in the US are covered under article 85, which does not require a showing of dominance. Moreover, even under article 86 the test for dominance occasionally seems designed to permit inquiry into practices by firms which in any broad sense have no appreciable market power. The clearest example is probably the Hugin case,[25] where Hugin was found to be dominant in the market consisting of spare parts for Hugin cash registers. The finding of dominance seems clearly motivated by the Commission's disapproval of Hugin's behaviour in refusing to supply spare parts to a single repair firm specializing in servicing Hugin's machines.

The Difference between the Second and Third Modes: Raleigh Bicycles

The difference between the second and third modes of enforcement can be illustrated with reference to the recent MMC decision involving Raleigh bicycles[26] in which the MMC condemned Raleigh's efforts to keep its bicycles out of discount stores. Under the second mode, the focus would be on the economic impact of Raleigh's conduct. Raleigh would be expected to provide a detailed explanation of its marketing programme and explain how its policy was necessary to maintain effective interbrand competition. This was much the same kind of argument that Raleigh made in its case before the MMC, and it is questionable whether it would have been any more successful in the US at that time. Despite the increasingly more relaxed attitude in the courts towards vertical restraints over the past ten years, the argument that Raleigh needed to avoid discounters so as to maintain its premium image (which seemed to be the heart of Raleigh's motives for the restraints) would have been regarded as having no strong connection with economic efficiency.

[24] See, for example, Merkin and Williams (1984, pp. 135–49).
[25] For a discussion, see Merkin and Williams (1984, especially p. 138).
[26] *Bicycles* (1981–82), HC 67.

Under the third mode, however, Raleigh's primary line of argument would be that the level of interbrand competition is vigorous (especially from imports), Raleigh has no significant individual market power, the industry is not highly concentrated, and the use of similar restraints is not widespread in the industry. There is thus no danger of Raleigh using the restraints to extract supra-normal profits and no risk that parallel use of the restraints by most firms in the industry could facilitate horizontal collusion among the manufacturers. Hence, there need be no inquiry into the actual mechanics of Raleigh's operations or speculation as to how consumers might be harmed. The inquiry would be relatively short and, from the facts available, it is likely that Raleigh would be successful.

Problems in the Use of Market Power as a Screening Device

Inferring Market Power from Conduct

Unfortunately, if a market power filter is to be of any real practical significance, the definition of market power or the method of assessing whether market power exists must be rigorous. In particular, if evidence of bad conduct can be used as the basis for an inference of market power, there is a danger that the purpose of the filtering process will be subverted, and the inquiry boils down completely to an analysis of conduct. Thus, for example, in the Hugin case the European Commission identified what it perceived was an abusive practice by Hugin in refusing to supply parts to independent repairers of Hugin cash registers, and in essence concluded that since Hugin had the power to engage in abuse, it must be dominant in some market, here identified as the market for Hugin's spare parts.

Yet the Commission seemed not to appreciate the possibility that Hugin's dominance in the spare parts market carried with it little or no market power. The Commission may have believed that owners of Hugin cash registers would be worse off due to the restriction in the number of alternative sources of repair. But if this were so, one would expect consumers to be less interested in purchasing Hugin cash registers in the first place. The European Court noted that the market for cash registers was very competitive and that Hugin had only a relatively small share, yet neither the Commission nor the Court seemed interested in pursuing that observation to its logical economic conclusion. Specifically, if Hugin's activities do in fact make owners of Hugin cash registers worse off, Hugin will suffer in the market for new cash registers and the problem will be self-correcting.[27]

It is worth repeating that the theoretical basis for the third mode of enforcement is not that firms without market power are incapable of misallocating resources or injuring consumers. It is rather that, in general, firms facing competition from other products have no incentive to behave in a way that systematically injures consumers *combined with* the fact that firms which do behave in this perverse way (perhaps out of malice or miscalculation) will be disciplined by the market.

Thus in the Hugin case, for example, proponents of the third mode of enforcement would not deny that the plaintiff suffered some injury as a result of Hugin's refusal to supply him with spare parts (although they might be more optimistic about the firm's prospects of re-establishing itself as a repairer of other makes of cash registers for which parts were available). However, they would argue that there is no need to drag out the complex (and expensive) antitrust machinery to deal with a problem that is essentially self-correcting from a competitive perspective. The dealer would be limited to possible contractual remedies and, if none was available, would be well advised not to allow himself in the future to become so dependent on a single supplier without contractual protection.

To take another example, suppose one observed a firm charging prices that apparently did not cover incremental costs. Suppose further that the available structural evidence did not indicate that the firm in question possessed market power or was likely to obtain it as a result of its pricing strategy, perhaps because its apparent market share was too low or because there were no perceivable barriers to entry. As a matter of theory, it could be argued that such behaviour is irrational unless it is likely to lead to monopoly, and the pricing behaviour would be taken as evidence from which one could infer that monopolization was a genuine risk, and that the structural evidence might be in error.

Advocates of the third mode of enforcement, however, would be more likely to resist making inferences about structure from the evidence on conduct, and would be more prepared either to conclude that the firm

[27] In the US a similar case involved the refusal of a computer manufacturer to license its operating system software except to purchasers of its central processing units. Despite the manufacturer's overall low market share in the market for computers, it was found to have market power over those customers who, owing to prior purchases, were 'locked in' to the particular manufacturer's software, and could, thereby coerce those customers into buying additional hardware. (*Data General Corp.* v. *Digidyne Corp.*, no. 84–761, US Supr. Ct., *cert. denied*, 1 July 1985.)

was behaving in a way that was economically irrational or, more likely, to raise a question about whether prices and incremental costs had been measured accurately by the observer who alleged that prices were below costs. In either case there would be no enthusiasm for intervening in the situation, since either the behaviour is not misallocative at all or, if it is (i.e. prices are in fact below incremental costs), it is self-correcting. This is not to say that, in close cases, conduct evidence can never be used to inform conclusions about market power. But, in general, the objective structural evidence would be weighted quite heavily, and if it showed an absence of market power, there would be a strong presumption that none existed.

The Interaction between Conduct and Measures of Market Power

The rationale for a structural screen, in which conduct is ignored, is weakened if the analytical methods for assessing market power are prone to error – especially to false negatives (concluding that a firm does not have market power when in fact it does). The rationale breaks down entirely if it is impossible to assess market power *without* considering conduct. How robust are the methods for assessing market power, and are those methods in any way dependent on an analysis of conduct?

The traditional method of assessing market power has been to define a product and a geographic market and to measure percentage shares attributable to different firms. A high share by one firm was taken to indicate market power. The method was criticized in the past by economists as excessively static and as frequently leading to the conclusion that market power existed when, in fact, there was little evidence that the firm in question had the power to price supra-competitively or otherwise behave in an anti-competitive fashion. However, there seemed to be no alternative method that was superior and, for the most part, economists were able to do no more than propose various *ad hoc* adjustments to the traditional method.

In 1982, however, the Justice Department Merger Guidelines (revised again in 1984) were published. These retained the basic outer framework of the market-definition/market-share approach, but contained a radically different method for actually defining the market and measuring market shares.[28] The method was primarily forward looking rather than historical, and was organized around the key question, 'What

[28] See Hay and Reynolds (1985) for a fuller discussion of the methodology and an illustration of the methodology in the context of a real merger.

would happen if there were only a single seller of product X and it attempted to raise price above the competitive level?' To what extent would consumers switch to other products (i.e. demand substitution)? To what extent would producers of closely related products (from a supply-side perspective) be able to switch to the production of X, and how many sales would they make (i.e. supply substitution)? To what extent would producers of X in other geographic regions be able profitably to ship into the sales territory of the producer in question, and how many sales would they make?

If, on the demand side, enough consumers would switch to a substitute product for the hypothetical price increase to be unprofitable, the relevant product market is broadened to include the substitute(s) and market shares are measured with respect to the broader market. For questions of supply substitution and geographic substitution the methodology is somewhat different. Producers of related products (on the supply side) are awarded 'imputed' market shares based on the amount of product X they would make and sell were the hypothetical price increase put into effect. Similarly, producers of X in different geographic regions are awarded an imputed share based on what they could profitably export into the territory of the firm in question. The result of these adjustments is that firms with historically high market shares of a given product may find their simulated market shares reduced below the level normally associated with market power, and the inference of market power is defeated.

Unfortunately, the approach breaks down when the firm or firms under examination are already exploiting market power. That is, if a firm is already charging a price 100 per cent above the competitive level, it is simply not relevant to the issue of whether that firm has market power to observe that if it attempted to raise price 20 per cent higher, it would lose most of its sales. The problem may not be serious when analysing mergers (since it can often be safely assumed that prior to the merger the industry is behaving competitively), and this is of course the primary orientation of the Guidelines.

However, the problem is potentially fatal if the question is whether a single firm does in fact possess market power. If the firm does, and has been exploiting that power in the form of supra-competitive prices or otherwise, the Guidelines' methodology gives unreliable answers. Firms will appear to face vigorous competition from imports (from nearby territories or other countries) or from firms who have taken advantage of supply substitutability to switch into production of the product in question.

However, instead of preventing exploitation of apparent market power, this new-found 'competition' is the result of the fact that genuine market power has been exploited.[29]

Because of this reversed flow of interaction between structure and conduct, it is impossible to give a definite answer to the question of whether a firm has market power without some information on how that firm is currently behaving. Firms which appear to face significant competition at any prices above present levels may none the less enjoy market power if current prices are too high, either in the sense that the firm is earning monopoly profits or in the sense that the firm is operating inefficiently such that the current costs contain a substantial component of waste.

To guard against the possibility that a firm is exploiting market power by charging supra-competitive prices, it appears necessary either to evaluate the firm's prices directly (e.g. by examining the relation between price and incremental costs) or to do so indirectly by looking for excess profits.[30] Neither method is particularly attractive. The relevant incremental costs for the purposes of assessing market power are long-run costs, which include more than simply the directly attributable out-of-pocket costs for labour and materials. Put differently, if the test was whether prices exceeded out-of-pocket costs for labour and materials, quite a substantial number of firms would be accused of enjoying monopoly power. Measuring the size of the gap between price and out-of-pocket costs is not conclusive either, since the margin over direct costs in competitive industries will differ widely as a function of capital intensity and other factors.

[29] This problem is sometimes referred to as the 'Cellophane trap' since in a major monopoly case against du Pont, virtually the only domestic seller of Cellophane, the Supreme Court noted that at du Pont's current prices the cross-elasticity of demand was high between Cellophane and apparent substitutes; the Court consequently broadened the market to include those substitutes, with the result of taking du Pont's market share well below the level normally associated with monopoly. The Court failed to consider the possibility that the high cross-elasticity may have resulted from the fact that du Pont was already charging monopoly prices. For a discussion of this case and a suggestion for how to resolve the analytical problems that may arise in such a situation, see Landes and Posner (1981).

[30] There is no obvious test for whether a firm is charging non-competitive prices due to inefficiency, since profits will not appear unusually high. It is reasonable to suspect, however, that the problem of inefficiency is largely confined to those monopolists insulated from the threat of competition by regulation rather than those monopolies that must continually 'earn' their dominant positions by offering consumers lower prices (or better products) than smaller rivals or new entrants.

Identifying excess profits is similarly difficult. For one thing, there are some real pitfalls in trying to convert profits as shown on the accountants' ledgers to the kind of data that would be useful to an economist.[31] But the problems in using reported profits as a signal of monopoly power go beyond difficulties such as the kind of accounting that causes profits to be understated in some years or overstated in others owing to the allocation of long-lived factors like advertising. Even if the reported profits are genuine, they cannot necessarily be associated with monopoly. In any given year, many firms make substantial profits, and there is no necessary reason to associate such profits with monopoly. Profit can be associated with luck, with skill, or simply with the short-run disequilibrium of an industry.[32]

If the profits persist over a long period, it is more difficult to argue that the explanation is simply short-run disequilibrium (although in an industry with rapid technological change there could be a series of short-run disequilibria, one after the other). However, it is possible that the profits are attributable not to monopoly but rather 'to ownership of a unique and long-lived asset that provides lower cost but does not confer monopoly power'.[33] Indeed, even if the profits continue over a period of years, they could still be attributable to superior skill, unless one makes the period long enough to be useless from a policy perspective.[34]

In short, it is necessary to know whether the profits are high despite competition or because of the absence of it. No simple numerical test based on the level of profits or the number of years they persist seems capable of providing a consistently accurate answer to that question. Indeed, the problems with using profits as a test for monopoly are seen by Franklin Fisher to be so serious that 'there is no way in which one can look at accounting rates of return and infer anything about relative economic profitability or, *a fortiori*, the presence or absence of monopoly-profits.'[35]

[31] See the discussion by Fisher et al. (1983, chapter 7) and the analysis of Fisher et al.'s arguments by John Kay in this volume.
[32] I occasionally find it useful to ask students (who are accustomed to associating high profits with monopoly power) to make a list of the ten most profitable firms (based on rate of return on equity) out of the Fortune 500 in each of the past ten years.
[33] See the discussion in Schmalensee (1982).
[34] That is, if profits persist for 50 years, superior skill alone seems an implausible explanation, but those charged with enforcing competition policy cannot wait 50 years to decide whether it is superior skill or not.
[35] Fisher et al. (1983, p. 253).

126 GEORGE A. HAY

To borrow from an old joke, 'the situation sounds hopeless, but is it serious?' At this point it is useful to recall that the role of the market power test in the third mode (and, effectively, in the second as well) is primarily to serve as a screening mechanism to decide whether to go to the next step of a detailed examination of conduct in order to determine if it is anticompetitive. This suggests that at least a partial solution to the problem of how to interpret excess profits is not to attempt to make the distinction between profits earned despite competition and those earned because of its absence.

That is, where the structural data suggest the strong possibility of monopoly, and analysis shows excess profits (after making whatever accounting corrections are feasible and reasonable), the best course may be to pass on to the next stage and examine the alleged anticompetitive conduct. If the conduct is found anticompetitive, then the presumption could be made that the situation will not be corrected naturally and policy intervention is appropriate. This does not eliminate the possibility that intervention will have been unnecessary (because in the absence of market power competition will have corrected the problem) or unwarranted (because the behaviour, while seeming suspicious, is in fact an efficient response to the business environment), but may reduce the risk to an acceptable level.

Whether such an approach can work depends upon the possibility of an independent assessment of conduct to determine whether it is anticompetitive. Where, however, the case is a straightforward monopolization case, and the conduct being challenged is the very fact of excess prices, the circularity is complete. One cannot then avoid the dilemma of having to distinguish between high profits that result from the absence of competition and high profits that are earned despite the presence of vigorous competition. That is to say, there is no other conduct which is being examined to determine whether it is anticompetitive. Happily, this is not a problem under US law, since excess profits are not sufficient to violate the antitrust laws, and some other kind of anticompetitive conduct is required as well.

Conclusion

This paper has considered the role of structure in evaluating firms' conduct, especially for those situations involving the behaviour of only a single firm as opposed to situations involving horizontal agreements. The major policy question is whether an analysis of market structure, in which the firm under examination is found to have market power, should be a necessary precondition for evaluating the firm's conduct under the antitrust laws. In the absence of market power, no detailed analysis of conduct would occur; that is, individual firms without market power can do anything they wish (excluding, of course, horizontal agreements) without offending antitrust laws.

If such a policy were adopted in the US – and there are some indications that US antitrust enforcement is moving in that direction – issues of market power would occupy the centre stage. An auxiliary question, therefore, is whether the methods for assessing market power are sufficiently robust to implement such a policy in the confidence that any resulting anticompetitive conduct would be ineffective and/or short lived. In at least some circumstances, it was suggested, the market structure methodology is insufficiently foolproof, with the result that such a complete *laissez-faire* policy is not without risks.

Notwithstanding some doubts about the wisdom of complete adoption of a structural screening mechanism for the US, there is sufficient merit in the underlying analysis for the UK and the EEC to be well advised to consider the advantages of at least a limited version of the structural screen, so as to give greater freedom to firms which are not dominant under any economic measure of dominance which focuses on interbrand competition. Antitrust authorities in those jurisdictions can also learn much from the previous mode of US enforcement, in which, for firms with market power, conduct is not condemned merely because it solidifies or enhances market share. Rather, an independent analysis of conduct is performed to determine whether the reason for the success is simply because the firm's conduct benefits consumers, without misallocating resources in either the short or the long run. There is nothing inherently misguided in a policy under which conduct for firms with market power is evaluated in this way, while the identical conduct for firms without market power is ignored. It is recognized, however, that such an enforcement policy would constitute a sharp break from current patterns.

References

Areeda, P. and Turner, D. F. 1975: Predatory pricing and related practices under section 2 of the Sherman Act. *Harvard Law Review*, 88, 697–733.
Bork, R. H. 1978: *The Antitrust Paradox*. New York: Basic Books.
Brodley, J. F. and Hay, G. A. 1981: Predatory pricing: competing economic theories and the evolution of legal standards. *Cornell Law Review*, 66(4), 738–803.

Easterbrook, F. E. 1984b: The limits of antitrust. *Texas Law Review*, 63, 1-40.

Fisher, F. M. McGowan, J. J. and Greenwood, J. E. 1983: *Folded, Spindled and Mutilated*. Cambridge, Mass.: MIT Press.

Hay, G. A. 1985: Vertical restraints. *Fiscal Studies*, 6, 37-50.

Hay, G. A. and Reynolds, R. J. 1985: Competition and antitrust in the petroleum industry: an application of the merger guidelines. In F. Fisher (ed.), *Antitrust and Regulation: essay in memory of John J. McGowan*, Cambridge, Mass.: MIT Press.

Hurwitz, J. and Kovacic, W. 1982: Judicial analysis of predation: the emerging trends. *Vanderbilt Law Review*, 35, 63-157.

Joskow, P. L. and Klevorick, A. K. 1979: A framework for analyzing predatory pricing policy. *Yale Law Journal*, 89, 213-70.

Landes, W. M. and Posner, R. A. 1981: Market power in antitrust cases. *Harvard Law Review*, 94, 937-83.

Merkin, R. and Williams, K. 1984: *Competition Law: antitrust policy in the United Kingdom and the EEC*. London: Sweet and Maxwell.

Schmalensee, R. 1982: Another look at market power. *Harvard Law Review*, 95, 1789-816.

Telser, L. G. 1960: Why should manufacturers want fair trade? *Journal of Law and Economics*, 3, 86-105.

Utton, M. A. 1979: *Diversification and Competition*. Cambridge: Cambridge University Press.

Utton, M. A. 1985: Predatory pricing and competition policy. Unpublished paper.

5

Assessing Market Dominance Using Accounting Rates of Profit

J. A. KAY

Introduction

Over 20 years a literature has developed which seeks to cast doubt on the way in which antitrust authorities use high accounting rates of return as a screening device in identifying potential cases for scrutiny. It suggests that accountants use conventions which are economically inappropriate, and hence that accounting rates of return cannot be treated as indicators of economic profitability. Perhaps the most extreme expression of this view is that of Fisher and McGowan (1983):

> There is no way in which one can look at accounting rates of return and infer anything about relative economic profitability or, *a fortiori*, about the presence or absence of monopoly. . . . The literature which supposedly relates concentration and economic profit rates does no such thing, and an examination of absolute or relative accounting rates of return to draw conclusions about monopoly profits is a totally misleading enterprise.

The purpose of this paper is to consider how accounting information might be used by those who are concerned to identify and act against market dominance. This issue is approached in two ways. First, the paper asks: what is the concept of economic profitability which would be relevant to an antitrust authority? Although it might seem that an answer to that question would be an essential preliminary to analysis supporting the assertions of Fisher and McGowan, it is not a question which appears to be addressed anywhere in their article or elsewhere. Having defined such a concept – which I call the economic rate of return – I then consider how accounting rates of profit are related to it.

However, it is apparent that antitrust authorities are not interested in high profitability as such. They are concerned because they think it may indicate entry barriers, or abuse of a dominant position, or some other characteristic of market structure, conduct, or performance. We might therefore, dispense altogether with the concept of economic profit, and ask: what inferences, if any, can be made about market conditions on the basis of high accounting rates of return? In this way we address directly the problem posed by Fisher and McGowan's remarks.

Profitability Criteria

The starting point for any assessment of economic profitability is the *internal rate of return* (IRR) on a project. The IRR is that rate of return which equates to zero the present value of the net cash flows, positive and negative, over the life of an investment. Capital expenditure is treated as a negative cash flow and hence no depreciation concept is employed. The *accounting rate of profit* (ARP) of a firm is calculated by reference to the profit, net of depreciation, generated in any accounting period: it is the ratio of that profit to the book value of the assets of the firm, net of depreciation.

Thus the IRR relates to a single project, and is calculated over the whole life of that project. The ARP relates to a firm – a collection of assets and projects – and is measured at a single time. Given the fundamentally different purposes of the two measures, it is not immediately apparent what relationship between the two one might expect to find.

The technique adopted by Harcourt (1965), Fisher and McGowan (1983), and others is to take a collection of projects all with the same internal rate of return and to show that the 'firm' so created will only in special cases report an accounting rate of profit equal to that internal rate of return. This is hardly surprising. A more realistic example would be one in which a firm undertakes many activities, commenced at different times, each with different internal rates of return. The outcome will be an accounting rate of profit varying over time. We are therefore faced on the one hand with a dispersion of rates of return on projects, and on the other with a dispersion of rates of profit over time. The sort of relationship we might hope to establish is that, in some appropriate sense, the average of these rates of return is equal to the average of these rates of profit. This is precisely the relationship which does indeed hold.

In order to establish that, we need to build bridges between the two distinct concepts of IRR and ARP. First, we need to generalize the IRR to describe a firm rather than a single project. Clearly, we could treat the aggregate cash flows derived by the firm as if they were those of a project, and hence derive an IRR for the firm over its whole life. Equally clearly, this is not a measure of economic profitability which an antitrust authority would find helpful. First of all, it is most unlikely that the authority has data extending over the whole life of a firm. Secondly, even if it did it would not yield answers to relevant questions. Once the firm had died, we might be able to establish that it had earned excess profits over its lifetime. We would not know when it had earned excess profits; we could not know in sufficient time; and we would have no way of knowing whether our antitrust policy had been successful.

Antitrust authorities are interested in profits over a finite segment of the life of a firm; indeed, the kinds of firm which attract their attention rarely die. Thus we should direct our interest to rates of return over segments. A rate of return can be computed over a segment if, and only if, we impute initial and terminal values to the firm's capital stock. For the purposes of an economic rate of return, these should be economic values – that is, an asset is to be valued at the present value of the expected earnings derived from it. Given these, and net cash flows during the period, the *economic rate of return* (ERR) is the internal rate of return which discounts to zero the stream of returns which would be obtained if the firm began the period by purchasing its assets for their economic value and ended it by selling on the same basis.

The *accounting rate of return* (ARR) is defined in a similar way over a segment of the life of a firm. The firm is assumed to buy its assets for their book value at the commencement of the segment. Over this period it derives net cash flows equal to its net accounting profit from its activities, and adds to its capital stock an amount equal to its gross investment less depreciation. At the end of the segment it sells the assets for their book value. The accounting rate of return is the yield at which this series of transactions breaks even. In contrast to the IRR and ARP, the ERR and ARR are concepts that seek to describe much the same thing. We go on to consider the relations between them.

Economic Rate of Return

The concept of the economic rate of return (ERR) requires further elaboration and exploration. Central to the calculation of an ERR is an estimate of the present value of the initial (time T_1) and terminal (time T_2) capital stock. The calculation of present value requires the specification of an appropriate discount rate. I assume here, and throughout the paper, that there is an exogenously given cost of capital ϱ. The issues involved in determining the cost of capital to a firm are already the subject of an extensive literature which will not be discussed further here. The prospective earnings from the stock of assets owned by the firm are then discounted. This capital stock refers to the assets actually held at that date, and the economic value is computed by discounting their expected net return at the cost of capital. Such a valuation may therefore differ from the economic value of the *firm*, which might include anticipated profits from assets which the firm has not yet purchased; and also from the economic value of a *project*, which is often computed by discounting future returns at the project's own internal rate of return.

Like the internal rate of return, the economic rate of return computed up to T_2 depends on cash flows subsequent to T_2. However, while the internal rate of return requires projections of costs and revenues from assets which the firm intends to purchase after T_2, the economic rate of return considers only prospective cash flows from assets already owned at T_2. Moreover, the internal rate of return r requires a complete specification of cash flows subsequent to T_2 (in order to allow a solution for r); the economic rate of return needs only knowledge of their present value at the cost of capital, and there may be external information which is helpful in assessing these magnitudes.

It should be noted that even if all the projects undertaken by a firm were to have the same internal rate of return, it would not necessarily be the case that this would be equal to the economic rate of return earned by the firm in any particular segment of its life. The reason for this is that if a firm undertakes a project with a yield in excess of the cost of capital, the computation of economic rate of return credits the firm immediately with a profit equal to the difference between its cost and its net present value. This is a deliberate and desirable characteristic of the economic rate of return, and one which is very much at the heart of the differences between economic and accounting concepts of profit. The economist treats profit as accruing when the profit opportunity is recognized: the accountant acknowledges it only when it is realized. This implies that if a firm creates a monopoly it may, at least in part, enhance the profitability of the firm during the period of creation rather than during the period of exploitation.

There is also another complication. The economic rate of return in a segment will depend not only on the profitability of the projects which the firm undertakes, but also on the rate at which new projects are commenced relative to the rate at which old ones are terminated. It follows from this that even in the standard case of Harcourt (1965) or Fisher and McGowan (1983), where *all* the component projects of the firm earn the same internal rate of return, this will not necessarily be the economic rate of return in any particular segment of the life of the firm. Of course, if the universal internal rate of return is the cost of capital, the rate at which the firm adopts new projects is irrelevant to its profitability and the economic rate of return is continuously also equal to the internal rate of return and the cost of capital. More generally, the economic rate of return will exceed the cost of capital by an amount which partly reflects the extent to which the average IRR exceeds the cost of capital, and partly reflects the rate at which new projects are undertaken. These relationships are explored in more detail in the appendix. If the firm is in steady-state growth, and there is a general internal rate of return applicable to all underlying projects, two propositions emerge

The ERR and IRR lie on the same side of the cost of capital.

The ERR is an increasing function of the rate of growth if the IRR is above the cost of capital.

These results and relationships should arouse suspicion that some of the alleged discrepancies between the ARP and the IRR result, not from divergencies between accounting and economic rates of profit, but from divergencies between economic rates of return – ERR and IRR – themselves. Such suspicions are well founded, as subsequent sections of this paper will show.

Accounting Rate of Return

The previous section considered the significance of the ERR: I now explore more carefully the construction of the ARR. The ARR is considerably influenced by the accounting conventions employed because of its dependence on the book value of assets. There are two principal asset valuation conventions – historic cost and current cost. Current cost accounting, having received considerable attention in the inflationary 1970s, is now in retreat: I shall suggest, however, that it is particularly appropriate for antitrust authorities.

Under historic cost accounting, assets are valued at original cost less some depreciation allowance which is itself based on original cost. Asset lives are normally selected conservatively and depreciation schedules may employ straight line, reducing balance, or other conventions. Before incorporating historic cost value in the balance sheet, however, an accountant must compare it with the economic value of the asset. The economic value is in turn the higher of the present value of earnings from the asset in its present use (its present value (PV)) and the disposal value of the asset (its net realizable value (NRV)). If the economic value is less than depreciated original cost then this lower valuation should be substituted.

Current cost conventions are similar except that replacement cost – the price of an equivalent modern asset – is used instead of historic cost. With inflation, replacement cost will normally exceed historic cost. Technological change may lead to replacement costs which are below historic cost, but in that instance it is likely that competition in the market will drive economic value below historic cost. If economic value is below replacement cost, then economic value should be substituted. Replacement cost accounting is a method extensively supported by academic accountants, but recently described as 'a practical technique in search of a theoretical rationale' (Whittington, 1983). The theoretical rationale is derived from the fact that it is replacement cost which determines the price of new entry. That is why current cost accounting is particularly significant for antitrust authorities.

One further accounting convention is of importance. Double-entry bookkeeping rules require that balance sheet changes should be matched to transactions in the profit and loss account. I shall interpret this as implying that all changes which affect asset values are taken through the profit and loss account. This is not always so: some movements in assets may be taken directly to reserves. Valuation changes of this kind need to be identified in appraising accounting information.

Return on Individual Projects

Although the primary focus of this paper is on the profitability of firms, consideration of rates of return on individual projects is a useful preliminary. In the single-project case, we need consider only the accounting rate of profit (varying over its lifetime) and the internal rate of return (characteristic of the project as a whole). The following individual-project results are now well known (Kay, 1976; Kay and Mayer, 1986):

1 If the accounting rate of profit is constant over the life of the project, it is equal to the internal rate of return in the project regardless of the depreciation conventions employed.

It is improbable that the firm will happen to have chosen depreciation conventions such that the ARP is constant. It may be, however, that it is remunerated in such a way that this happens automatically. Examples would include: non-competitive government contracts, where the contract price is fixed so as to include a prescribed return on (accounting) capital employed; and industries subject to rate of return regulation. In both these cases, projects which fall within the scope of the fixed accounting regime will have IRRs equal to the predetermined ARP.

2 The IRR is equal to the average ARP, when the average profit rate is weighted by the book value of capital employed discounted at the average ARP.

In addition to establishing the general relationship between IRR and ARP, this enables the IRR on a project to be computed directly from accounting data.

We may also be concerned to rank projects. One possible basis for doing so is suggested by the following result:

3 If there are two projects such that one always reports accounting rates of profit greater than i and one always reports profit rates below it, then the more profitable project also shows a higher internal rate of return.

One value of i which is of particular significance is ϱ, the cost of capital. From this we have:

4 If the accounting rate of profit is always greater than the cost of capital, so is the internal rate of return.

Return over Segments of a Firm's Life

Our principal interest, however, is not in the lifetime of projects but rather in segments in the life of firms. One relevant result is immediate, however, as an application of result 2:

5 The accounting rate of return over a segment in the life of a firm is equal to the average accounting rate of profit, weighted by book value discounted at the average ARP.

and we can immediately deduce from this:

6 If the average ARP (weighted by book value discounted at the cost of capital) is greater than the cost of capital over some segment, so is the ARR.

J. A. KAY

If the segment of the life of a firm which we observe is a complete segment – it covers the whole of the life of the firm so far – then a number of strong results are now available. Consider the relationship between the ARR and the ERR over such a segment. The initial value of capital stock is the same – zero – for the compilation of both ARR and ERR. The terminal value of capital stock is the book value for purposes of computation of ARR and the economic value for purposes of computation of ERR. Economic value is at least as great as book value; and so ERR is at least as great as ARR, which is in turn equal to average ARP. Two corollaries follow:

7 If, over the life of a firm so far, the average ARP is greater than the cost of capital, so is the ERR.

8 If, over the life of a firm so far, the ARP has been greater than the cost of capital, so has been the ERR.

These results are true under either historic or replacement cost conventions, or indeed any accounting principles which rule out asset valuations above economic value.

From this, we can immediately obtain some help in assessing returns in particular segments. Suppose a firm, citing Fisher and McGowan (1983), queries the antitrust authority's examination of a period during which the ARR exceeded the cost of capital. Then the authority can reply that, to use this defence, the firm must be able to identify a period during which the ARP was below the cost of capital. If it can do this, the authority may still infer that the ERR is above the cost of capital if, taking the two periods together, the average ARP remains above it. Thus the referee of Fisher and McGowan's paper who suggested that IBM was more profitable than American Motors – presumably having observed that IBM had always earned a higher ARP – was, of course, perfectly correct.

The Steady-State Firm

It is improbable that we could obtain any completely general results on the relationship between ARR and ERR over a segment in the life of a firm. Historic cost accounting conventions give an opportunity for a firm to depreciate its assets very rapidly, relative to their physical deterioration, during some particular period, and this will benefit future ARPs at the expense of depressing current ones. Such practices are not uncommon.

Such problems would not necessarily arise, however, if the firm were consistent in its behaviour, where consistency refers to two aspects: the depreciation bases applied to any specific asset category, and the stock of assets held by the firm. A firm in steady-state growth maintains a balanced stock of assets: if, at the same time, it applies the same depreciation schedules to any particular newly purchased asset, then its behaviour is consistent in both these senses. We then have:

9 For a firm in steady-state growth, if the ARP exceeds the cost of capital so does the ERR.

A proof of this is given in the appendix. It follows from it that a firm which claims that a high ARP is a misleading indicator of its ERR must show that current experience is exceptional, by reference to variation in the scope or pace of its investment programme or changes in its approach to depreciation rules.

Contestable Markets

Outside approximate steady states, we have seen less prospect of stable relationships between ARP and ERR. It may be better to consider the direct question of what light high ARPs, or ARRs, shed on market conditions. It is apparent that accounting valuation rules, particularly those of current cost, are related to these conditions. Two are of particular interest. *Free entry* to an industry implies that present value is no greater than replacement cost, since otherwise entry to depress present value will occur. An *absence of sunk costs* implies equality of replacement cost and net realizable value.

If both conditions – free entry and an absence of sunk costs – hold then the market is *contestable*. Since only firms for which present value is at least as great as net realizable value will exist, contestability implies equality of present value, replacement cost, and net realizable value. In a contestable market, therefore, current cost asset valuations are always based on present value and it follows that *ex ante* returns, and *ex post* returns if expectations are fulfilled, will always be equal to the cost of capital. The effects of uncertainty, and the prospect of deviations between *ex ante* and *ex post* rates of return, are discussed in Kay and Mayer (1986): here I assume that returns are correctly anticipated.

If there are no sunk costs, then the book value of assets will always be based on their replacement cost. If the observed accounting rate of profit over a segment is greater than the cost of capital, it must be the case that economic value at the beginning of the segment was greater than replacement cost. It therefore follows that:

10 If there are no sunk costs, and the average cost accounting rate of return over a segment in the life of a firm exceeds the cost of capital, entry to the industry was blocked at the beginning of that segment.

If there is free entry at the end of the segment, then book value at the end of the segment will reflect economic value. If the ARP over that segment exceeds the cost of capital, it must be the case that economic value at the beginning of the segment exceeded book value, and hence entry was blocked. Thus we have:

11   Even if there are sunk costs, an average current cost accounting rate of return in excess of the cost of capital implies that entry was blocked either at the beginning or at the end of the segment.

Finally, taking these results together, we have:

12 In a contestable market, the current cost accounting rate of return is always equal to the cost of capital.

Conclusions

What inference can antitrust authorities make if they observe accounting rates of return in excess of the cost of capital? The results of this paper fall into three main categories:

Regardless of the accounting conventions employed   Over the whole life of the firm, the average accounting rate of profit is equal to the rate of return on the firm's activities taken as a whole.

If the firm uses either historic cost accounting or a replacement-cost-based CCA system   If the average accounting rate of return exceeds the cost of capital over the firm's active life so far taken as a whole, the economic profitability of its activities also exceeds the cost of capital. If the firm is in steady-state growth for a segment of its life, and the accounting rate of profit exceeds the cost of capital, so does its profitability.

If the firm uses replacement cost accounting   If the average accounting rate of profit over a segment of the life of the firm exceeds the cost of capital, then if the market in which it operates is contestable, entry was blocked at the beginning of that segment; if it is not contestable, entry was blocked at either the beginning or the end of that segment.

Thus the common practice of using high accounting rates of return in the preliminary scrutiny of industries which are the subject of market dominance is a wholly appropriate one. Current cost accounting systems using 'value to the business' rules are particualrly relevant for antitrust purposes and their adoption should be encouraged. More generally, the difficulties of using accounting data for these purposes are the result not of underlying deficiencies in economic concepts, but of the problems in applying these concepts in practice.

Appendix

This appendix demonstrates formally a number of assertions about the steady-state properties of the economic rate of return, ERR, made earlier.

For a firm in steady-state growth undertaking projects which yield the IRR, the ERR exceeds the cost of capital if and only if the IRR does

Suppose the projects which the firm undertakes cost k and yield a net amount $f(t)$ at a time t after inception until their economic life ends at time y. The IRR (r) on these projects is therefore defined by

$$k = \int_0^y f(t)e^{-rt}dt$$

The firm in steady-state growth undertakes investment e^{gT} at date T. The value of an asset installed time x ago is

$$\int_x^y f(t)e^{-\varrho(t-x)}dt$$

and the quantity of such assets owned at date T is $e^{g(T-x)}$. Hence the economic value of the firm's assets at T is

$$W(T) \quad \equiv \int_0^y \int_x^y e^{g(T-x)} f(t)e^{-\varrho(t-x)} \, dt \, dx$$

$$= e^{gT} \int_0^y \int_x^y e^{(\varrho-g)x} f(t)e^{-\varrho t} \, dt \, dx$$

Let

$$\phi(x) \quad = \int_x^y f(t)e^{-\varrho t}dt$$

Then

$$We^{-gT} \quad = \int_0^y \phi(x)e^{(\varrho-g)x}dx$$

$$= \frac{1}{\varrho-g} \left| \phi(x)e^{(\varrho-g)x} \right|_0^y - \frac{1}{\varrho-g} \int_0^y \phi'(x)e^{(\varrho-g)x}dx$$

$$= \frac{1}{\varrho-g} \left[\int_0^y f(x)e^{-gx}dx - \int_0^y f(x)e^{-\varrho x}dx \right]$$

Let $F(T) \quad \equiv \int_0^y e^{g(T-x)}f(x)dx = e^{gT} \int_0^y f(x)e^{-gx}dx$

and $k(y) \quad = \int_0^y f(x)e^{-rx}dx$

and hence, by analogy with $F(T)$

$$K(T) \quad \equiv e^{gT} \int_0^T f(x)e^{-rx}dx$$

It follows that

$$\frac{F-K}{W} \quad = (\varrho-g) \frac{\int_0^T f(x)e^{-gx}dx - \int_0^T f(x)e^{-rx}dx}{\int_0^T f(x)e^{-gx}dx - \int_0^T f(x)e^{-\varrho x}dx}$$

$$= (\varrho-g)\lambda$$

From the definition of the economic rate of return, $\bar{r}$

$$\bar{r}W = (F-K) + \dot{W}$$

where $\dot{W}$ is the derivative of W with respect to time. By the assumption of steady-state growth $\dot{W} = gW$, so that

$$\bar{r} = \frac{F-K}{W} + g$$

We consider only cases where $g < \varrho, r$, so that the firm has finite present value. With $g < \varrho, r$, then if $r > \varrho$, $\lambda > 1$ and so

$$\bar{r} = \lambda\varrho + (1-\lambda)g < \lambda\varrho + (\lambda-1)\varrho = \varrho$$

Similarly if $r<\varrho$, $\lambda<1$ and

$$\bar{r}=\lambda\varrho+(1-\lambda)g<\lambda\varrho+(1-\lambda)\varrho=\varrho$$

and if $r=\varrho$, $\lambda=1$ and $\bar{r}=\varrho$. Hence

$$\bar{r}\gtreqless\varrho \quad \text{as} \quad r\gtreqless\varrho$$

The ERR decreases with the rate of steady-state growth if the underlying IRR exceeds the cost of capital

Since $\bar{r}=\lambda(\varrho-g)+g$,

$$\frac{d\bar{r}}{dg}=(\varrho-g)\frac{d\lambda}{dg}+(1-\lambda)$$

Since $\dfrac{d\lambda}{dg}<0$, $\dfrac{d\bar{r}}{dg}<0$ if $\bar{r}, r>\varrho$

If the steady-state ARP is greater than the cost of capital, so is the ERR

The authority may have data for a limited segment of the firm's life during which it has been in steady-state growth. During that period, the ERR is given as

$$\bar{r}W=gW+(F-K)$$

and the ARP (which is equal to the ARR over any steady-state segment) is given as

$$aV=(F-D)$$

where D is accounting depreciation.

With the firm in steady state, the book value of assets (V) also grows at rate g so that

$$gV=K-D$$

and hence

$$\frac{\bar{r}-g}{a-g}=\frac{W}{V}$$

Since $W\geq V$ and assuming, as before, that r, $\varrho>g$ so that firms have finite present value, this implies that $\bar{r}\geq a$. Hence for a firm in steady-state growth, the economic rate of return is greater than the accounting rate of return. It follows that if the ARP exceeds the cost of capital, so does the ERR.

Bibliography

Baumol, W. J., Panzar, J. C. and Willig, R. D. 1982: *Contestable Markets and the Theory of Industry Structure.* New York: Harcourt, Brace, Jovanovich.

Fisher, F. M. and McGowan, J. J. 1983: On the misuse of accounting rates of return to infer monopoly profits. *American Economic Review*, 73, 82–97.

Flemming, J. S. and Wright, J. F. 1971: Uniqueness of the internal rate of return: a generalisation. *Economic Journal*, 81, 256–63.

Franks, J. R. and Hodges, S. D. 1983: The meaning of accounting numbers in target setting and performance measurement: implications for managers and regulators. Unpublished paper.

Harcourt, G. C. 1965: The accountant in a golden age. *Oxford Economic Papers*, 17, 66–80.

Kay, J. A. 1976: Accountants too could be happy in a golden age: the accountant's rate of profit and the internal rate of return. *Oxford Economic Papers*, 28, 447–60.

Kay, J. A. and Mayer, C. P. 1985: Interdependence and value to the business rules. Unpublished paper.

Kay, J. A. and Mayer, C. P. 1986: On the application of accounting rates of return. *Economic Journal*, 96, 199–207.

Whittington, G. 1983: *Inflation Accounting.* Cambridge: Cambridge University Press.

6

Do Dominant Firms Decline?

P. A. GEROSKI

Introduction

There appears to be a widespread presumption amongst economists that it
is the fate of dominant firms to decline. A subject of frequent discussion
in the 1950s and early 1960s, it appears (with one or two exceptions)
to have remained just below the surface of collective consciousness
since then. The thesis of this paper is that a critical examination of the
empirical evidence indicates that the presumption of decline is based on
extremely weak foundations. Dominant firms do decline, but the notion
that there is anything quick, systematic, or inevitable about it is doubtful.

There are several reasons why one might find these results of interest.
First, we know little about how fast markets work. Most economic
theory focuses on long-run equilibrium positions, and what is neglected
is an analysis of how long it might take to arrive at such positions from
various starting points. Since our results suggest that markets do not
work fast, some reorientation of theorizing seems to be in order.
Secondly, the result that 'dominant firms do not decline (very fast)' is
worrying from the point of view of antitrust policy. While it is not always
obvious that dominant firms should (from a social welfare point of view)
decline, this kind of empirical result does mean that, in general, we
cannot expect market processes to break up dominant positions quickly

I am grateful to Rob Masson for helpful discussions prior to the first draft, to the
hospitality of the IIM in Berlin, to participants at the market dominance conference for a lively discussion, and to Dick Allard, Tony Buxton, Roger Clarke,
Steve Davies, Bob Feinstein, Donald Hay, Tim James, Dennis Mueller, Rob
Porter, Mike Scherer, Richard Shaw, Richard Schmalensee, Geoff Shepherd,
Margaret Slade, and John Vickers for helpful comments on an early draft. The
usual disclaimer applies.

when restructuring is necessary. Antitrust decisions will have to include explicit allowances for the time that markets take to work when the opportunity cost of intervention is computed. The sluggishness of market processes may indeed provide ample justification for intervention.

Our examination of the empirical evidence is in two stages. First, we examine the actual record of the decline of market leaders in the US and the UK.[1] While data such as this are suggestive, they are often difficult to interpret. We have, therefore, constructed a counterfactual description of a competitive process to use in evaluating the data. The second stage of our examination focuses on a particular hypothesis associated with the presumption of decline, which arises from certain price leadership models and suggests that prices will be set to manage or regulate the rate of decline. The evidence that we shall examine tends to cast much doubt both on the proposition that there is, in general, a substantial decline in the market positions of dominant firms, and on the hypothesis that, when decline occurs, it is a consequence of such profit-maximizing or 'managed' decline strategies. This leaves one with the problem of accounting for the decline that is observed; to this end, alternative views are given by way of a very brief and extremely impressionistic reading of some of the evidence.

Assessing the Hypothesis of Decline

The hypothesis that 'dominant firms decline' is one element of a broad presumption that market processes work well, eliminating positions of monopoly power and asymmetric market structures which are based on an incomplete diffusion of the information necessary to improve efficiency. The basis of this presumption is, of course, a notion that entry and intra-industry mobility are generally unrestricted in markets, and work as mechanisms which react to and regulate the level of returns earned by competitors.

[1] There is a debate (which need not concern us here) concerning the appropriate definition of dominance. A market share of 40 per cent is the conventionally accepted cut-off point, although it is arguable that, in defining a dominant firm by its market share, one is defining a cause by its consequence. For further remarks in this vein (which, however, lead to nothing immediately operational), see Geroski and Jacquemin (1984); Ono (1981) is also interesting in this regard.

Yet, however reasonable it seems at face value, this presumption is much too vague to work with. Stated in its simplest form as the hypothesis that 'dominant firms decline', it is almost impossible to reject. Every observed decline in the market share of leading firms would be consistent with the hypothesis, however trivial, transitory, or glacial it might be, and any observed decline is sufficient to ensure that it is not rejected. Most economists would not wish to contemplate a hypothesis stated in such an uninteresting form (or one so prone to measurement errors), and would wish to add all or part of 'noticeably, quickly, and permanently' to the end of the assertion. That is, by 'decline' most would read 'substantial decline'. Whilst this makes the hypothesis somewhat more acceptable in content, it remains untestable until one has decided how much decline in what time is reasonably consistent with it. Answering this requires one to be more specific about the workings of the kind of market processes which underly the assertion. This we shall do in a fairly simple way, using a three-equation model that can be fairly easily related to published empirical work.

To model the hypothesized process of decline, we first presume that its market position enables a dominant firm to earn excess profits. Let $S(t)$ be the market share of the dominant firm at the time t, and let $\pi(t)$ be its profits. We suppose that

$$\pi(t) = \alpha + \beta S(t) \tag{1}$$

where $\alpha, \beta > 0$. Secondly, we take entry and intra-industry mobility by non-dominant firms – collectively $E(t)$ – to be attracted by such excess returns with, say, a one-period lag; we suppose that

$$E(t) = \mu + \eta \pi(t-1) \tag{2}$$

where $\mu, \eta > 0$. Finally, the consequence of entry is the erosion of the market share of the dominant firm and all other industry incumbents not clever enough to expand, say in the proportions θ and $(1-\theta)$ respectively. That is,

$$\theta E(t) = -[S(t) - S(t-1)] \tag{3}$$

where $\theta \epsilon [0,1]$.

It is often the case that one cannot observe the forces which generate market dynamics. In this event it is useful to combine equations (1)–(3) to yield a simple autoregression in an observed variable like $S(t)$:

$$S(t) = \varrho S(t-1) + \epsilon \tag{4}$$

where $\varrho = (1 - \theta\eta\beta)$ and $\epsilon \equiv -\theta(\mu + \eta\alpha)$.[2] Obviously, no decline occurs if the dominant firm is unaffected by entry: $\theta = 0 \Rightarrow \varrho = 1$, $\epsilon = 0$. If entry does not respond to profits ($\eta = 0$) then $\varrho = 1$, but decline can occur if there is exogenous entry: $\mu > 0 \Rightarrow \epsilon < 0$. Finally, if the dominant firm makes no excess profits because of its high market share ($\beta = 0$) then $\varrho = 1$, but (again) decline will occur if excess profits are made independent of market share ($\alpha > 0$), and either endogenous or exogenous entry occurs: $\mu, \eta > 0 \Rightarrow \epsilon < 0$.

The object of constructing a model like (1)–(3) is to develop a feel for how noticeable, quick, and permanent a market share erosion has to be in order to be consistent with the hypothesis that dominant firms experience the kind of substantial decline we associate with the workings of competitive markets. A very rough and ready description of a competitive process might be as follows: $\alpha = 0$, $\beta = 0.5$, $\mu = 0.05$, $\eta = 0.8$ when time is measured in units of five years, and $\theta = 0.5$.[3] These parameter values imply that $\varrho = 0.8$ and $\epsilon = 0.025$. Table 6.1 shows the projections of the dominant firm's market share based on these conjectures. The process described in table 6.1 is not terribly fast, at least when $\epsilon = 0$, but excess profits are at least halved within 15 years or so. As long as it is impossible to imagine a truly competitive market operating more slowly

[2] The precise details of the lag structure of the model need not concern us here. They are obviously important in deriving the precise shape of (4), but eliminating the lag to make (2) a contemporaneous relationship will not eliminate the autoregressive character of (4), although it will slightly affect the interpretation of ϱ and ϵ. In the latter case, $\varrho = (1 + \theta\beta)^{-1}$ and $\epsilon = -\theta(\mu + \mu\alpha)(1 + \theta\beta)^{-1}$

[3] I have constructed this counterfactual as follows. Equation (1) can be interpreted via standard models of maximizing behaviour (see for example Saving, 1970) for a derivation using the dominant firm pricing model to be discussed below). If, say, pricing is Cournot and the industry demand elasticity is equal to 2, then $\alpha = 0$. $\beta = 0.5$. The value of $\theta = 0.5$ is based on the notion that entrants are equally likely to take sales from dominant firms as from other incumbents (for simplicity, we assume that θ is fixed; this random theft assumption actually implies $\theta(t) = S(t)$). μ reflects exogenous entry, that is entry unrelated to excess profits. Imagine a process in which outsiders randomly come across new ideas that enable them to enter and challenge incumbents: 5 per cent penetration over five years does not seem unreasonable for non-major innovations. Finally, $\eta = 0.8$ is based on the notion that excess profits ought to attract perhaps up to ten entrants from the pool of potential entrepreneurs over a five-year period, each getting no more than 2 per cent of the market when excess profits are as high as 25 per cent. Whether or not this seems reasonable hinges on how large one thinks the pool of potential entrepreneurs is; if it is large, then one expects η to be larger than 0.8.

Table 6.1 Evolution of the counterfactual competitive industry

1 Years	2 $S(t)$	3 $S(t\ )$
Initial	0.5000	0.5000
5	0.4000	0.3750
10	0.3200	0.2750
15	0.2560	0.1950
20	0.2048	0.1310
25	0.1638	0.0798
30	0.1310	0.0388
35	0.1048	0.0235

Column 2 is calculated from parameter values $\varrho = 0.8$ and $\epsilon = 0$; column 3 is calculated from $\varrho = 0.8$ and $\epsilon = 0.025$.

or ineffectually than this, then table 6.1 will serve our purposes in what follows.

The evidence we have consists primarily of multiple observations on the market shares of dominant firms over time.[4] Before using table 6.1 to interpret this data, however, it is worth briefly examining some econometric estimates of the parameters of equations (1)–(3). While somewhat indirect (in that they are not gleaned only from observations concerning markets containing dominant firms), such estimates nevertheless do contain information germane to establishing the relevant counterfactual.

Equations like (1) and (2) have been estimated several times in the literature, although most of the evidence that we have comes from the US. A reading of the literature suggests that the values $\beta = 0.2$, $\eta = 0.5$, and $\theta = 0.9$ are not untypical, although it must be emphasized that the last figure is based on very sketchy evidence.[5] Together these numbers

---

[4] One could also consider data describing turnover at the top amongst the leading firms in the economy; e.g. Scherer (1980, pp. 54–6) contains a succinct survey of this type of study. We have not considered these data here as our definition of dominance refers to market and not aggregate shares (see footnote 1).

[5] I have arrived at these numbers as follows. For equation (1), I examined the literature on the relation between market shares and profits. Martin (1983) generated numbers (corrected here for a change in units) of 0.095, 0.098, 0.0685, and 0.0707 in various regressions; Kwoka (1979) found that the firm with the leading share attracted a coefficient of between 0.193 and 0.0317; Gale (1972) found coefficients in the 0.080, 0.098 range; Ravenscroft (1983) estimated β to be between 0.183 and 0.1476; and, finally, Shepherd (1972) uncovered relatively

imply $\varrho = 0.91$, and table 6.2 charts their implications for a dominant firm with an initial market share of 0.5.[6]

It is clear that far more time is required for dominant firms to shed market share on table 6.2 than was the case for table 6.1. If no exogenous

---

high coefficients in the 0.2396, 0.5235 range. Leaving out Shepherd, a guesstimate of $\beta = 0.1$ might be reasonable; including Shepherd and allowing for the possibility that some of the many other variables in these regressions could be mistakenly attracting market share effects leaves us at $\beta = 0.2$. Shepherd (1975) uses estimates of $\alpha = 6$, $\beta = 0.25$ to calculate what he calls an 'imputed degree of market power' in a context related to (1). For equation (2), we have only two studies using entrants' market share as the dependent variable. Using the same body of data, both Harris (1976) and Masson and Shaanan (1982) generated estimates of just under $\eta = 0.5$ in a model with a lag of six to eight years. There is reason to think that this might overstate the true effect, for virtually all other entry studies (which use specifications in which the dependent variable is something like the natural log of the change in the number of firms in the industry) generate values of $\eta = 0$ (see Gorecki, 1976; Orr, 1974; Baldwin and Gorecki, 1983; and Khemani and Shapiro, 1983, who are virtually the only ones who found η significantly different from zero, although their estimated value of η was extremely small). Placing low weight on the second group of studies gives the estimate in the text – a number somewhat smaller than those published because of the shorter lag used in the text. The only evidence we found on (3) comes from Biggadike's study of successful entry by large firms which suggested that θ is nearly unity (see Biggadike, 1979, chapter 10). My feeling is that the 'true' values of η and θ are below those of the text, and so the 'true' value of ϱ is larger than 0.91; i.e. that the econometric numbers used in the text unduly favour the hypothesis. This gives added support to the conclusions drawn below.

[6] It is also possible to compare the implied values of $E(t)$ in the various scenarios with observed data. On table 6.1, we expect $E(5) = 0.20$, $E(10) = 0.16$, and so on for column 2, and $E(5) = 0.25$, $E(10) = 0.20$, and so on for column 3. On Table 6.2, the pairs for columns 2 and 3 are $E(5) = (0.05, 0.10)$ and $E(10) = (0.095, 0.093)$. What is surprising about direct observations on entry is how low entry apparently is. Masson and Shaanan's (1982) sample averaged 4.5 per cent market share for entrants in six to eight years. Yip (1982) looked at 59 entrants to narrowly defined US markets and observed an average market share gain of 10 per cent (the median was 6 per cent); the initial gain for direct entry was 2.3 per cent (for entry via acquisition, the corresponding figure was 6.3 per cent). Biggadike (1979) examined 40 entry attempts by 20 large US firms. Most had aspirations of gaining at least 10 per cent market shares (again, the definition of markets seemed to be rather narrow) within two years, and nearly 40 per cent achieved this goal. He observed little share growth in the first four years after entry, however; shares tended to increase thereafter at a slow rate. Hause and du Reitz (1984) examined entry in Sweden over a 15-year period: new entrants averaged 5.8 per cent penetration and (surprisingly) diversified entrants a 1.7 per cent penetration. These numbers seem to be more consistent with the values of table 6.2 than those of table 6.1.

Table 6.2 Evolution of the 'real world'

1 Years	2 $S(t)$	3 $S(t)$
Initial	0.5000	0.5000
5	0.4550	0.4300
10	0.4141	0.3663
15	0.3767	0.3083
20	0.3428	0.2555
25	0.3120	0.2075
30	0.2839	0.1638
35	0.2583	0.1240

Column 2 is calculated from parameter values $\varrho = 0.91$ and $e = 0$; column 3 is calculated from $\varrho = 0.91$ and $\epsilon = -0.025$.

entry occurs, then it takes 35 years on table 6.2 to halve the dominant firm's initial market share; in the counterfactual this occurred in 15 years (20 and 10 respectively if exogenous entry is allowed). While not ideal for use in testing the hypothesis that concerns us here, these econometric estimates are nevertheless informative. They suggest that decline is indeed likely to occur, but only at a glacial pace. Those who are willing to see the numbers displayed on table 6.1 as a reasonable characterization of the competitive process will, accordingly, be tempted to view table 6.2 as evidence which is, at the very least, somewhat inconsistent with that counterfactual.[7]

A second type of evidence is somewhat more direct, taking the form of several time series observations of the market shares of individual

---

[7] One can rearrange (1)–(3) into an autoregression in profitability of the form $\pi(t) = \lambda \pi(t-1) + \epsilon'$, where $\lambda \equiv \varrho$, $\epsilon' = \beta\epsilon + (1-\varrho)\alpha$. Models of this type are, of course, useful to analyse when observations on $E(t)$ are lacking (see for example Geroski, 1985), and some estimates for the US are available in Mueller (1986), for the UK in Cubbin and Geroski (1985), and for the UK, France and Germany in Geroski and Jacquemin (1985). In general, the estimated values of λ tend to be lower than the value of $\varrho = 0.91$, although this is for samples largely involving firms with market shares a good deal less than 40 per cent. One might hazard the guess that $\lambda < \varrho$ could reflect a greater transitory element in monopoly rewards than in monopoly positions, especially for rewards not based on dominant positions, and this is consistent with Mueller's observation that λ is higher for firms with larger market shares.

dominant firms. For this, the representation of equations (1)–(3) in the form of equation (4) is relevant.

Shaw and Simpson (1985a) examined two samples of dominant firms in the UK. The first was a sample of 28 firms whose history they traced for between 9 and 13 years following investigation by the Monopolies and Mergers Commission. From an initial average market share of 60.2 per cent, 22 of the 28 experienced some decline (5 actually increased their share), 5 declined by at least 20 per cent, the average decline was 8.4 per cent, and the median decline was 6 per cent. The authors also examined a second group of 19 firms over at most 15 years (they were a control group not investigated by the MMC). Their average initial market share was 42.1 per cent, the mean and median declines were 4.1 and 2 per cent, with only 12 of 19 actually exhibiting a decline (for some further details, see the appendix). Roughly the same story emerged from Pascoe and Weiss's (1983) study of a group of dominant firms in the US 1950–75. Focusing on 27 five-digit (SIC) industries with matching market definitions in 1950 and 1975, they observed 23 firms which had at least 40 per cent of the 1950 market. Of these, 14 experienced a decline, with an average erosion of about 7.4 per cent. Shepherd (1975) collected information on dominant firms in the US for two different periods, 1910–35 and 1948–75 (reproduced here in the appendix). In the period 1910–35, 17 of 20 firms declined, registering an average decline of 25.6 per cent over 25 years; in the period 1948–75, 11 of 18 registered decline, and an average decline of 18.1 per cent was observed.

Thus the evidence takes the form of information about 108 dominant firms in the US and the UK.[8] Of these, 32 did not decline. Further, between 46 and 51 firms registered declines of 6 per cent or less; this seems to have been the case for 22–4 of the UK firms over 9–13 years, and for 24–7 of the US firms over 25 years. So 30 per cent of the sample is clearly inconsistent with the hypothesis of decline, and only 20–30 per cent of the sample registers declines that are sufficiently large and fast to be clearly consistent with the process sketched in table 6.1. Were the

[8] The sample of firms used by Caves et al. (1984) and a number of cases cited by Scherer (1980) suggest that some dominant firms formed during the turn of the century merger wave failed rather quickly. This implies that the survivors who persisted in dominant positions long enough to make it into our three samples import a distinct sample selection bias to our numbers, exaggerating the degree of persistence. The sample of 108 firms also exaggerates our information since not all of the Shaw-Simpson firms meet the 40 per cent initial criterion, and since there may be some overlap in the Weiss-Shepherd samples.

hypothesis true, it is most unlikely that numbers of this order of magnitude would have been generated by chance.

Taken together, both sets of empirical evidence do not appear to provide very compelling support for the hypothesis. The data on market share erosion are hardly impressive evidence in favour; interpreted against the benchmark of table 6.1, they are fairly impressive evidence against. Similarly, the econometric work does not paint a picture of market processes rapidly eroding the shares of leading firms. Clearly, the numbers suggest that dominant firms do decline. Just as clearly they banish the notion that there is anything quick and systematic about such declines. It is in this sense that one can confidently reject the hypothesis that 'dominant firms decline noticeably, quickly, and permanently'.

The Hypothesis of Optimally Managed Decline

The notion that 'dominant firms decline' is a presumption that follows naturally from a certain type of price leadership model. This describes a scenario that we shall call the hypothesis of 'optimally managed decline'. Expounded in classic papers by Worcester (1957), Gaskins (1971), and others, the argument goes roughly as follows. Entrants are attracted to markets (at an increasing rate) by signals such as the current price or profits enjoyed by incumbents. When they arrive, they behave as price-takers and they free-ride on the benefits of the output restriction created by the dominant firm's pricing policies. The dominant firm has open to it the single option of a price strategy which involves the trade-off of high prices and profits today against the low profits tomorrow caused by the response of entrants to today's prices. The optimal policy in the face of this trade-off is to moderate current prices somewhat to regulate the flow of entry; when the dominant firm has no cost advantage, this policy involves gradually and gracefully yielding market share to entrants.

Whatever one thinks of it on *a priori* grounds,[9] the notion of optimally managed decline does claim some empirical support, the case of US

---

[9] There are three sorts of reservations one might muster to this argument. The first is that the argument artificially restricts the dominant firm to following a price policy. There are, of course, numerous other strategies open to incumbents facing entry, and the use of many of them can block entry or pre-empt entrants (e.g. see the survey by Geroski and Jacquemin, 1984). Secondly, it is difficult to know why entrants respond to prices in the fashion posited. Any kind of substantial or lumpy entry requires the entrant to examine post-entry (not pre-entry) prices and, indeed, it is not clear why entrants considering their challenges do not

Steel being a prominently cited example. Restricting our attention only to those cases where a substantial decline has occurred fairly quickly in the position of a leading firm (or group), we must decide how to go about examining the hypothesis of optimally managed decline, i.e. the assertion that decline arises because this type of price leadership occurs. Several methodological difficulties arise. First, there is the question of how many examples are needed to make the case. This seems to be almost impossible to answer satisfactorily, and we propose to proceed as follows. Having found one or more examples which do seem to fit the hypothesis of managed decline, we examine other cases where decline occurred but not for the reasons posited by the hypothesis. We then move on to try and assess just how important pricing is as a post-entry weapon. We will reject the hypothesis if it is difficult to find examples of decline consistent with it, if it is easy to find examples inconsistent with it, and if, in general, price seems to be infrequently utilized by incumbents after entry. Such a rejection does not imply that optimally managed decline never happens; rather, it eliminates the presumption that optimally managed decline explains the majority of cases of decline.

The second difficulty with the hypothesis of optimally managed decline is in establishing what kind of evidence is decisive for or against it. The theory suggests that, following entry, prices will decline and price cuts will be used to slow the rate of growth of entrants' shares of the market. The difficulty is that observing such associations between pricing and penetration is not conclusive evidence. Consider the obvious alternative hypothesis of a dominant firm following a totally myopic strategy of setting short-run profit-maximizing prices in every period, neglecting the erosion of the market caused by this strategy. This yields a higher price in

---

take the same long-run view of the industry's prospects as do incumbents. More fundamentally, it is just not clear that current prices or the profits of incumbents convey the information on market demand, incumbents' costs, and so on, that a well-founded entry attempt requires. Finally, the nature of competition – non-cooperative price leadership – used in the model is troubling. Other forms of price leadership exist (such as collusive or barometric price leadership) which do not entail the free-riding that is the crippling liability (in the long run) shouldered by the dominant firms in this model. In fact, this type of price leadership is actually rather undesirable in the sense that while all agents prefer there to be a price leader rather than not, they individually prefer others to take the mantle. In this sense, one can argue that it is the dominant firm itself which has been pre-empted in this model, and that 'price leadership in an oligopoly may be an unprofitable distinction evaded by the small firms and assumed perforce by the large one.' (Schelling, 1960, p. 23)

every period relative to the entry regulating price, but in all other respects the price paths of the two competing hypotheses will look the same. In particular, price will fall upon entry, and price cuts will be large when the entrants' collective market share rises rapidly. Evidently, the decisive evidence for or against the hypothesis concerns myopia and the willingness to trade current for future gains, and not just correlations between price movements and market penetration by entrants.

The most famous example of managed decline is claimed to be that of US Steel. Formed in 1901 by a giant merger which gave it 65 per cent of the production of steel ingots in the US, US Steel has steadily lost market share since. By 1967, it claimed only 24 per cent of the market (see e.g. Scherer, 1980, p. 239). Stigler (1965) examined the financial returns to investors in US Steel and in other steel companies and concluded that, in the period 1901–25 (when US Steel conceded about 24 per cent in market share), the holders of US Steel stock did better than investors in any other steel company save Bethlehem Steel. He argued that 'exploitation of shareholders did not take place'; that is, he rejected the hypothesis that the combine was formed to sell securities to untutored investors, in favour of the alternative that US Steel was formed to exploit monopoly power in the short run. 'The formation of US Steel must therefore be viewed as a master stroke of monopoly promotion.' (pp. 111–12) In evaluating the persuasiveness of Stigler's claims, one can certainly argue about whether these stock market returns may have reflected the pricing strategies for pig iron and not steel ingots (e.g. Parsons and Ray, 1975), and whether share valuations are good reflections of the capitalization of the future earnings of some initiative (compare Schiller, 1981). Further, it is not clear that stock market returns would have followed the Stigler pattern under a policy of managed decline. Faced with the knowledge that US Steel was merely postponing the inevitable decline (albeit in an optimal fashion), shareholders might have undervalued US Steel relative to those firms free-riding on its pricing policy. That Bethlehem Steel, a substantial beneficiary of US Steel's policy, was so valued is persuasive, but it was not the only beneficiary of the hypothesized pricing policy. Finally, it is not clear whether Stigler's calculations pick up more than the market's *changed expectations* about the value of the merger relative to its initial estimates in 1901. This view would suggest that his numbers show little more than that in 1901 the stock market did not overestimate the future returns to the formation of US Steel. In short, the test is at best far too indirect and ambiguous to be of any real use in evaluating the hypothesis.

Adams (1961) examined the pricing in this industry, and found evidence suggesting that US Steel undertook a leadership role in pricing, particularly with regard to price rises and restrictions on price-cutting. Vertical price squeezes (see also Adams and Dirlam, 1964) have been used in this industry against independent fabricators, and have led to exceedingly passive responses to imports (e.g. the prices of wire rods actually rose in 1955–9, a period of rapidly growing imports), but it is hard to see these as primarily responses to entry.[10] Managed decline certainly does not enter into the list of five causes of decline listed by Adams. The apparent neglect of entry in pricing policy may well have been due to US Steel's ability to control the supply of iron ore (by means of pricing and denying access to supplies; see for example Parsons and Ray, 1975). Indeed, US Steel's spectacular decline in steel ingots was definitely not matched by a loss of control of rich iron ore deposits.[11] Finally, one must not see in US Steel's decline a descent into vigorous industry competition, since it and Bethlehem Steel jointly controlled over 50 per cent of the market for a long period, and the industry still remains highly concentrated. A pattern of ceding market share only to a few large rivals is hardly consistent with the usual story of managed decline in the face of hordes of entrants, and may not add up to a market structure sufficiently deconcentrated to dislodge the industry from near-monopoly

[10] Indeed, it is in some ways hard to credit US Steel with the kind of long-term decision horizon needed to make a strategy of optimal decline attractive, in view of its apparent short-sightedness in the matter of introducing innovations like continuous casting and the basic oxygen furnace (e.g. Ault, 1973; Oster, 1982; Adams and Dirlam, 1966). I understand that US Steel was by no means so inefficient at the outset (e.g. its 1911 Gary works was said to be the most efficient at the time), although its administrative arrangements seem to have been somewhat loose (Chandler, 1977, p. 361). While disagreeing with Scherer, who sees US Steel as consistent with a strategy of managed decline, it is easy to agree with his view that: 'In the long run, competition does triumph. But, in the long run, when an industry behaves the way the US steel industry has behaved, the industry is likely to be moribund' (Scherer, 1983, p. 309).

[11] Scherer (1980, p. 240) remarks that Xerox followed a similar path in conceding the low-volume reproduction market to entrants following the expiration of its patent, and Kodak appears to have done the same in the UK (see later in the text). For further discussion of Xerox see Blackstone (1972) and Bresnahan (1985), the former of whom claims support for the notion of managed decline. What is not clear in Blackstone is whether such pricing was really a cause of decline. My reading of these studies suggests that Xerox could well have decided to abandon certain markets (to consolidate its position in others), and managed decline may well be a sensible way for it to implement such a decision.

pricing.[12] In short, regulation of entry into the steel industry may well have occurred, but probably it was largely through vertical price strategies. There is not much evidence to suggest that the prices of steel ingots were ever very far from their monopoly levels despite US Steel's precipitate drop in market share, and thus it is hard to see this example as solid evidence in favour of the hypothesis of managed decline.

While US Steel is unlikely to be one of them, it is possible to find examples which do seem to fit the hypothesis fairly well. One is presented by Shaw (1974), who examined the response to entry in the UK retail petrol market. The top two firms had 80 per cent of the market in the 1950s, dropping to about 60 per cent by the end of the 1960s. Shaw observed that three types of strategies towards entry were adopted by them: space packing and crowding out by buying up retail outlets; advertising; and a 'measured price response'. The last largely consisted of price cuts timed to coincide with striking advances in entrants' market shares – a correlation that Shaw interpreted as consistent with the hypothesis of managed decline. These price cuts also occurred during periods when the supply of petrol eased relative to demand, so it is clear that price cuts would have occurred to some extent in the absence of entry. Nevertheless, it seems plain that incumbents perceived entry threats and mounted replies, so myopia can be fairly confidently ruled out.[13] Hence, the observed price movements do seem to be consistent with the hypothesis.

[12] Shaw and Simpson (1985a) note that the decline of leading firms in their samples is rarely matched by a decline in the leading group of firms. If managed decline is implemented by the leading firm alone, this pattern is at best not inconsistent with the hypothesis; if, as seems not unlikely in highly concentrated industries, managed decline is implemented by the leading group, then this is clearly inconsistent. Some have seen American Can's decline as not inconsistent with managed decline, but since American Can leaked share largely to Continental Can, and since they clearly co-operated in pricing until at least the late 1950s (about 50 years after American Can's 95 per cent market share had begun to erode and about 20 years after it had hit 56 per cent), I am unable to see this claim (see Hessian, 1961).

[13] A slight reservation is as follows. Schmalensee (1978) argues that when firms have the option of space packing and advertising, it is not optimal for them to limit price. Hence, fearlessly using the imperfect analogy between limit pricing and entry regulation, one might argue that the evidence that retail petrol incumbents were space packing and advertising more or less rules out the interpretation of the observed pricing correlations as having anything to do with entry. This may be, but it does not seem overpowering.

Whilst it is admirable as a case study, Shaw's methodology is not as precise as one might wish. Potentially more direct and precise are explicit econometric applications of the Gaskins model, estimating unknown parameters in the first-order conditions describing price behaviour. Brock (1975) applied such a model to IBM, which experienced two periods of decline in market share (from 78 per cent in 1957 to 65 per cent in 1965, and from 75 per cent in 1968 to 67 per cent in 1971). He concluded that it was 'probably not in IBM's interest to let its market share decline' (p. 71), primarily because of the high industry growth rate. Hence, if one decided that one or both of these setbacks for IBM really was 'decline', the hypothesis of managed decline does not explain what happened. While Brock does cite pricing episodes from time to time that appear to be consistent with the hypothesis, it seems rather more likely that competition through the generation of new products is primarily responsible for much of the variation in market shares observed in this industry. Sengupta et al. (1983) also applied a Gaskins model to the US computer industry, comparing it explicitly with the alternative hypothesis of myopia. While they claim that the Gaskins model outperformed the myopic one, their predictions using the former seriously understate the fringe's output and profits (despite the fact that they computed trajectories from a point most favourable to the hypothesis of managed decline). While laudable in ambition and method, both applications to the US computer industry are less than convincing as evidence for the hypothesis.

We have explored several potential examples of managed decline (incidentally exhausting the various methods which have been used to examine it), and are left with one fairly persuasive example and two fairly unpersuasive ones.[14] It is one thing to find such examples, and another thing altogether to find them to be common. Furthermore, there are other instances of decline that have nothing to do with managed decline. There are cases where antitrust intervention can be credited with

[14] There are several further examples cited in Scherer (1980, pp. 239–42). Caves et al. (1984), Yamawaki (1985), Pascoe and Weiss (1983), Hannan (1979), and Masson and Shaanan (1982) all present and discuss economic results germane to the hypothesis under consideration. As a body of evidence, they are informative more on the factors which appear to be associated with decline than on the speed of decline or the pricing conduct which may (or may not) underlie it. They are also rather less precise and informative than the case studies on which we have chosen to focus here.

some impact on positions of dominance. Other causes of decline are also easily identified. Shaw and Simpson (1985b) discuss three examples. Fisons, whose share of the compound fertilizers market fell from 43 per cent in 1959 to 36 per cent in 1969, appears to have suffered from an inability to cope with the innovations introduced by entrants. Although there was a brief post-entry price war in 1969–70, this actually occurred well after a major entry by Shell and an intensification of ICI's activities in the early 1960s (see also Shaw, 1980, 1982). Kodak's 63 per cent share of the film process market in 1966 fell to 25 per cent by 1982 – a consequence of its decision to concentrate on selling equipment and materials to processors, and of a shift in demand from colour slides (which Kodak dominated) to prints (which it did not). Finally, Metal Box saw its market share drop from 94 per cent in 1968 to 31 per cent in 1982 after the expiry of various long-term agreements with US firms, and the cessation of a wide range of restrictive practices against entry which had protected it. Other examples exist where managed decline was not, apparently, profit maximizing. The end of entry protection through patents in polyester fibres led incumbents to adopt a strategy of accommodation with entrants, it being thought that the strategy of blocking would be too expensive in terms of forgone profits. The accommodation strategy did not entirely work, and some price competition did, in the event, break out (see Shaw and Shaw, 1977).

In fact, these and numerous other examples of decline suggest no more than that the sleepiness of dominant firms is often the principal cause of their undoing. Imperial Tobacco, long dominant in the UK, was remarkably slow to react in 1968 to widely anticipated changes in the tax on cigarettes and lost share to more alert smaller rivals (e.g. Prais, 1981, chapter 9). Dunlop, whose share of the tyre market dropped from 47 per cent in 1951 to 20 per cent in 1980, seems to have been slow to start producing radial tyres (e.g. Prais, 1981, chapter 16). The US ready-to-eat cereal producers, ever ready to proliferate brands to block entry, failed to anticipate the shifts in demand in the early 1970s that allowed entry into the natural foods segment of the market (e.g. Schmalensee, 1978; though share losses by leaders may have only been temporary in this case). Our impression is that one can find many examples of this type, especially by considering dominant firms exposed to international competition. These sorts of examples lead one to question whether the policy of managed decline is a *consequence* rather than a *cause* of decline. That is, for a firm taken by surprise and unable to block entry by various strategic actions, the policy of managed decline may prove to be an acceptable way to usher in the more or less inevitable declines caused by prior and more fundamental failures.[15]

There is one final body of evidence that is relevant, which is information on how incumbents typically respond to entry. The hypothesis of managed decline is very much a story involving price and, indeed, decline is at least partly a reflection of the weakness of this type of competitive weapon relative to various pre-emptive investments that incumbents could make. The evidence that we have on the response by incumbent firms to entry suggests that price is not often a weapon of real importance for incumbents, dominant firms or otherwise. Yip (1982), in his study of direct entry and entry by acquisition, found very little response by incumbents to direct entry challenges, and none at all to entry by acquisition (p. 118). Biggadike (1979) found that, in 45 per cent of the entry challenges he observed, no incumbent reaction was forthcoming at all; of the remaining 55 per cent in which some reaction was noted, three-quarters showed no price response. That is, in only 13 per cent of cases did he observe a price response which might be even loosely consistent with the hypothesis. Case studies reveal a similar picture. Golden Wonder's attempt at entry to the UK potato crisp industry (Bevan, 1974) in the early 1960s was met eventually by heavy advertising and the introduction of flavoured crisps by Smiths. Smiths seems to be another example of a sleepy dominant firm who declined, their complacency partly created by confusing increased revenue in a growing market with the maintenance or increase of market share. Incumbents in the UK dry cleaning industry were slow to respond to the flood of entry occasioned in the late 1950s and early 1960s by changes in the technology of dry cleaning machines. Their eventual response – massive defensive investment to convert their facilities – did lead to a price war, but largely of a predatory variety to reduce excess capacity by driving out entrants (Shaw, 1973). Entry into the UK domestic washing machines market (Shaw and Sutton, 1976) did not provoke a price response as much as retaliation by advertising and product innovation. This also seems to be the characteristic feature of response to entry in the computer industry, with IBM frequently adopting a fast-second strategy in reply to imitative

---

[15] See also the earlier discussion in footnote 10. It has, however, been suggested that a consequence of the passive pricing policy underlying managed decline is a proclivity to be surprised, to be sluggish in response to change, and so on. Applied, for example, to US Steel, the argument goes: 'Because they implemented managed decline, they became (in due course) technological laggards', passivity in one dimension spreading to others.

and innovative product launches by entrants and rivals (Brock, 1975). These examples suggest that pricing is generally not a strategic weapon of great importance in post-entry battles. This, in turn, suggests that the applicability of the hypothesis of managed decline is rather limited.

To conclude, a firm not enjoying significant cost advantages and restricted to replying to entry largely by pricing is likely to set high initial prices and accept decline. It may, if it is sufficiently clever, do this in a manner which is consistent with the hypothesis of optimal managed decline. Examples of this phenomenon undoubtedly do exist. However, there are lots of examples which, at best, do not fit the restrictive *ceteris paribus* conditions surrounding the proposition of managed decline and, at worst, are inconsistent with it. Given that this is true for the rather small percentage of the dominant firm population which actually do decline, it is hard to sustain a faith in the presumption that managed decline is a common fate of market leaders. The best that one can say for the hypothesis of managed decline may well be the following. A firm fated to decline, because it has failed to pre-empt entrants or has decided to concentrate its resources elsewhere, may implement such a decline gradually, using price to regulate its erosion of share in a profit-maximizing manner. One hazards the guess that this possibility covers a number of the examples that we have found to be apparently consistent with the hypothesis.

Alternative Hypotheses

The analysis thus far has led us to the somewhat embarrassing position of having to explain an empirical outcome which we did not expect. The evidence suggests that dominant firms do occasionally decline, and that those that do may occasionally behave in the manner posited by the managed decline hypothesis. This leaves us with the problems of accounting for the decline of those firms who do not behave in this fashion, and of accounting for the persistence of those that do not decline. Attention accordingly shifts from 'do dominant firms decline?' to 'why don't they?'[16]

[16] One possibility can be noted straight away. It is possible that one does not observe decline in markets historically defined because entry challenges do not occur in these traditional arenas. In this view, dominant firms decline when markets shift out from underneath them. This idea is consistent with data presented by Gort and Klepper (1982), which suggest that entry plays a major role in affecting industry dynamics only in early phases of product life cycles. A second possibility

160   P. A. GEROSKI

In seeking to answer the second question, it is natural to start by observing that the original Worcester (1957) argument is really concerned with the long-term instability of the dominant firm market structure. His thesis was that the structure is unstable only in the absence of scale economies and absolute cost advantages. More generally, one can reasonably argue that mobility barriers of various types ought to be sufficient to insulate leading firms from the competitive incursions of rivals. It is certainly conceivable that these conditions are present sufficiently often in markets to make the instability hypothesized by Worcester as rare as our data suggest (for a survey of the evidence see Geroski, 1983). Yet this is more a description of how dominant firms persist than an explanation of why. The creation of mobility barriers requires a series of strategic decisions and actions – an alertness and competitive vigour – that must itself be explained, for mobility barriers are not exogenous in origin. That the persistence of dominant firms might prevail over decades of competitive interaction seems so implausible *a priori* as to demand an explanation.

Is it the case that dominant firms have both the ability and the incentive to take and maintain the lead in competitive races for market position? It is clear from recent theory (e.g. Geroski and Jacquemin, 1984) that there are numerous instances in which the optimal strategy for incumbents to follow is to pre-empt entrants altogether (by capacity expansion, product proliferation, patenting, and so on). To do this, incumbents merely have to remain alert, for these arguments suggest that the incumbent has an incentive to spend enough to win whatever competitive race the entrant provokes. This, in turn, suggests that the issue of persistence and decline hinges largely on alertness; dominant firms decline when they get sleepy and fail to pre-empt, and they tend to persist in leading positions otherwise because they can and will pre-empt if they are able to. In other words, these pre-emption arguments suggest that dominant firms have the *incentive* to take actions which ensure their persistence. Whether they have the *ability* to do so depends on whether the are alert enough to seize their opportunities. It is the latter point that demands attention.

---

that we shall not consider in the text is the argument that the seeds of decline are to be sought in the manner by which initial dominance was achieved. While it is clear that those dominant firms which faded very rapidly did so because of flaws in their construction (e.g. a too hasty set of mergers), it seems difficult to account for decline (or its absence) 25 to 50 years after creation mainly in these terms. It also seems easy to reject a popular variant of this argument, namely that dominance is determined largely by the lifespan of the initial promoter.

This then leaves one seeking to explain persistance in market positions largely by a persistent alertness in leading firms.[17] It is usual to argue that it is the competitive process which creates such alertness in firms, and it is important to be precise about what is meant by 'competitive' in this context. It is clear that one does not mean the absence of entry barriers, for there are examples of firms persistent in the presence of both high and low barriers. It is also clear that one does not mean the presence of entry, for while a dominant firm that declines usually does so owing to entry (or, at least, substantial intra-industry mobility), there are plenty of examples of dominant firms persisting in the face of entry attempts. What may well be the important feature of a competitive environment in this context is that entry is regular and innovative. It may be not entry challenges *per se* but their regularity that matters; it may be not the ability of entrants to replicate the activities of existing firms but their threats to introduce new and better ways of doing business that matters. In short what matters, on this view of competition, is not how many entrants as much as how often they enter and how innovative they prove to be.

On a fairly casual level, this view does claim some striking illustrations. A notable feature of the US computer industry is the regularity of entry and its frequently innovative nature. Yet IBM has persisted in occupying a leading position, pre-empting some entrants and playing a fast-second strategy against others. The feature of this case that separates it from some of the examples of decline that we have examined earlier is precisely this aspect in the challenge of entry; one is tempted to conjecture that it is largely because the entry challenges that IBM has had to face have been regular and innovative that IBM has remained alert. Similarly, vigorous product differentiation in the US car industry combined with the risks of styling failure have kept General Motors (and, indeed, the 'big three') fairly alert and innovative on the styling front. However, the leading car firms have been innovative only in those areas where competitive

[17] The hypothesis in the text hinges on the notion that competitive vigour is something largely determined by the external environment in which firms find themselves. An alternative view might stress internal factors. Firms frequently can follow up innovations with further innovations, successful managers can recruit and hire successful managers, and so on. All of this seems conceivable, but the argument is largely concerned with potentialities. Successful managers *may* have a comparative advantage in locating successful successors, good ideas frequently have the *potential* of generating more good ideas, and so on, but why is it that agents exploit these opportunities? The answer to this question seems to me to lie in the competitive pressures thrown up by the external environment.

challenges have pressured them. Thus, when forced to do so by imports, they have developed small cars, but they have dragged their feet on air pollution and safety standards. The weakening of entry challenges and the weak position of independents since the war has noticeably slowed the rate of advance in product technology (e.g. White, 1971). Finally, the apparent sleepiness of many giants (like US Steel) seems to have occurred in the absence of substantive entry challenges over lcng periods coupled with a sudden, well-organized attack.

The hypothesis that this line of reasoning leads one to is the following: *dominant firms decline when they become sleepy and thus vulnerable to a sudden, innovative entry challenge; and they become sleepy when they have not, over a reasonable period, faced such types of challenge.* Subject a firm continuously to regular and bracing challenges, and there is a good chance that it will survive and prosper; subject it to challenges only very irregularly, and there is a good chance that it will fail when one of them occurs. This alternative hypothesis on the dynamics of dominant firms is consistent with all the evidence that we have observed thus far. While this is admittedly not a very stringent test, it is at least more than can be said for the other hypotheses that we have examined in this paper.

Appendix

Tables 6.3 and 6.4 set out the Shepherd (1975) data. Columns 3 and 4 set out counterfactual estimates of terminal shares corresponding to $\varrho = 0.8$ and $\varrho = 0.91$ ($\epsilon = 0$ in both cases), i.e. comparable with tables 6.1 and 6.2. The data are clearly inconsistent with the process displayed on table 6.1; only two cases (10 per cent) on table 6.3 and none on table 6.4 register declines consistent with a process involving $\varrho = 0.8$, $\epsilon = 0$. The data even suggest slower erosion than that implied by the econometric estimates of table 6.3; eight and two firms (40 and 11 per cent) respectively fit a process in which $\varrho = 0.91$ and $\epsilon = 0$. Note, as pointed out by Shepherd, that there seems in these data to be a clear decline in the speed of market share erosion throughout the century.

Another way to interpret these data is in terms of half-lives. A process like equation (4) reaches a share of $S(\tau) = \varrho^\tau S(0)$ from a starting point $S(0)$ in τ years (if $\epsilon = 0$). The half-life T is given by $T = \log 2/\log \varrho$, or $T = 15.5$ years if $\varrho = 0.8$ and $T = 36.7$ years if $\varrho = 0.91$ (recall that t is measured in units of five years). Since only six (or 30 per cent) and one (5 per cent) of the firms on tables 6.3 and 6.4 have lost 50 per cent or more of their market shares in 25 years, it is clear that the implicit value of ϱ that describes their decline greatly exceeds 0.8 and probably exceeds 0.91.

After the text was completed I received from Richard Shaw the raw data from Shaw and Simpson (1985a). There is very little in them that would make me wish to alter the text but, for the sake of precision, it is worth briefly describing them. Only 30 of the 47 firms satisfy the 40 per cent initial share criterion. Of these 30, two saw their share rise, the average fall was 10.4 per cent (8.6 neglecting one outlying firm which fell 63 per cent in 14 years), and one-third had declines of less than 10 per cent over about 10 years. Eight firms fell below the 40 per cent cut-off point, but all but one were only marginal to start with; thus approximately 70 per cent of the sample retained dominance. The

Table 6.3 Dominant firms in the US, 1910–35 (per cent)

Company	1 Market share 1910	2 Market share 1935	3 Counter-factual 1935 share	4 Second counter-factual 1935 share
US Steel	60	40	19.7	37.4
Standard Oil	80	35	26.2	49.9
American Tobacco	80	25	26.2	49.9
International Harvester	70	33	22.9	43.7
Central Leather	60	—	19.7	37.4
Pullman	85	80	27.8	53.0
American Sugar Refining	60	35	19.7	37.4
Sugar Mfgr	75	55	24.6	46.8
General Electric	60	55	19.7	37.4
Corn Products	60	45	19.7	37.4
American Can	60	51	19.7	37.4
Westinghouse Electric	50	45	16.4	31.2
du Pont	90	30	29.5	56.1
International Paper	50	20	16.4	31.2
National Biscuit	50	20	16.4	31.2
Western Electric	100	100	32.8	62.4
United Fruit	80	80	26.2	49.9
United Shoe Machinery	95	90	31.1	59.3
Eastman Kodak	90	90	29.5	56.2
Aluminum Company of America	99	90	32.4	61.8

Table 6.4 Dominant firms in the US, 1948–75 (per cent)

Company	1 Market share 1948	2 Market share 1975	3 Counter- factual share 1975	4 Second counter- factual share, 1975
General Motors	60	55	19.7	37.4
General Electric	50	50	16.4	31.2
Western Electric	100	98	32.8	62.4
Alcoa	80	40	26.2	49.9
Eastman Kodak	80	80	26.2	49.9
Procter & Gamble	50	50	16.4	31.2
United Fruit	80	60	26.2	49.9
American Can	52	35	17.0	32.4
IBM	90	70	29.5	56.2
Coca-Cola	60	50	19.7	37.4
Campbell Soup	85	85	27.8	53.0
Caterpillar Trucks	50	50	16.4	31.2
Kellogg	50	45	16.4	31.2
Gillette	70	70	22.9	43.7
Babcock & Wilcox	60	50	19.7	37.4
Hershey	75	70	24.6	46.8
du Pont (cellophane)	90	60	29.5	56.2
United Shoe Machinery	85	50	27.8	53.0

average starting share was 66.23 per cent; terminal shares were 55.8 per cent on average. To be consistent with a process in which $\varrho = 0.8$ and $T = 2$ (or ten years), the average decline should have been 23.8 per cent (11.4 per cent if $\varrho = 0.91$). In fact, only one firm declined in a manner consistent with $\varrho = 0.8$ (ten were consistent with $\varrho = 0.91$).

References

Adams, W. 1961: The steel industry. In W. Adams (ed.), *The Structure of American Industry*, New York: Macmillan.

Adams, W. and Dirlam, J. 1964: Steel imports and vertical oligopoly. *American Economic Review*, 54, 626–85.

Adams, W. and Dirlam, J. 1966: Big steel, invention and innovation. *Quarterly Journal of Economics*, 80, 167–89.

Ault, D. 1973: The continued deterioration of the competitive ability of the US steel industry: the development of continuous costing. *Western Economic Journal*, 11, 89–97.

Baldwin, J. and Gorecki, P. 1983: Entry and exit to the Canadian manufacturing sector: 1970–79. Economic Council of Canada, unpublished paper.

Bevan, A. 1974: The UK potato crisp industry 1960–72: a study of new entry competition. *Journal of Industrial Economics*, 22, 281–97.

Biggadike, E. 1979: *Corporate diversification: entry strategy and performance.* Graduate School of Business Administration, Harvard University Press, Cambridge, Mass.

Blackstone, E. 1972: Limit pricing and entry in the copying machine industry. *Quarterly Review of Economics and Business*, 12, 57–65.

Bresnahan, T. 1985: Post-entry competition in the plain paper copier market. *American Economic Review*, 75, 15–19.

Brock, G. 1975: *The US Computer Industry: a study of market power.* Cambridge, Mass.: Ballinger.

Caves, R., Fortunato, M. and Ghemawat, P. 1984: The decline of dominant firms, 1905–29. *Quarterly Journal of Economics*, 99, 523–46.

Chandler, A. 1977: *The Visible Hand.* Cambridge, Mass.: Harvard University Press.

Cubbin, J. and Geroski, P. 1987: The convergence of profits in the long run. *Journal of Industrial Economics*.

Gale, B. 1972: Market share and rate of return. *Review of Economics and Statistics*, 54, 101–9.

Gaskins, D. 1971: Dynamic limit pricing: optimal pricing under threat of entry. *Journal of Economic Theory*, 3, 306–22.

Geroski, P. 1983: The empirical analysis of entry: a survey. University of Southampton, unpublished paper.

Geroski, P. 1985: The persistence of profits: some methodological remarks on measurement and explanation. University of Southampton, unpublished paper.

Geroski, P. and Jacquemin, A. 1984: Dominant firms and their alleged decline. *International Journal of Industrial Organization*, 2, 1–28.

Geroski, P. and Jacquemin, A. 1985: The persistence of profits: a European comparison. University of Southampton, unpublished paper.

Gorecki, P. 1976: The determinants of entry by domestic and foreign enterprises in Canadian manufacturing industries. *Review of Economics and Statistics*, 58, 485–8.

Gort, M. and Klepper, S. 1982: Time paths in the diffusion of product innovations. *Economic Journal*, 92, 630–53.

Hannan, T. 1979: Limit pricing and the banking industry. *Journal of Money Credit and Banking*, 10, 438–46.

Harris, M. 1976: Entry and barriers to entry. *Industrial Organization Review*, 4, 165–74.

Hause, J. and du Reitz, G. 1984: Entry, industry growth and the microdynamics of industry supply. *Journal of Political Economy*, 92, 733–57.

Hessian, G. 1961: The metal container industry. In W. Adams (ed.), *The Structure of American Industry*, New York: Macmillan.

Khemani, R. and Shapiro, D. 1983: Alternative specifications of entry models. Bureau of Competition Policy, Ottawa, unpublished paper.

Kwoka, J. 1979: The effects of market share distribution on industry performance. *Review of Economics and Statistics*, 61, 101–9.

Martin, S. 1983: Market, firm and economic performance. Monograph series in finance and economics, NYU Graduate School of Business Administration.

Masson, R. and Shaanan, J. 1982: Stochastic dynamic limit pricing: an empirical test. *Review of Economics and Statistics*, 64, 413–23.

Muller, D. 1986: *Profits in the Long Run*. Cambridge: Cambridge University Press.

Ono, Y. 1981: Price leadership: a theoretical analysis. *Economica*, 49, 11–20.

Orr, D. 1974: The determinants of entry: a study of the Canadian manufacturing industries. *Review of Economics and Statistics*, 61, 58–66.

Oster, S. 1982: The diffusion of innovation among steel firms: the basic oxygen furnace. *Bell Journal of Economics*, 13, 45–56.

Parsons, D. and Ray, E. 1975: The US steel consolidation: the creation of market control. *Journal of Law and Economics*, 18, 181–220.

Pascoe, G. and Weiss, L. 1983: The extent and performance of market dominance. Federal Trade Commission, Washington DC, unpublished paper.

Prais, S. 1981: *Productivity and Industrial Structure*. Cambridge: Cambridge University Press.

Ravenscroft, D. 1983: Structure – profit relationships at the line of business and industry level. *Review of Economics and Statistics*, 61, 22–31.

Saving, T. 1970: Concentration ratios and the degree of monopoly. *International Economic Review*, 11, 139–46.

Schelling, T. 1960: *The Strategy of Conflict*. Cambridge, Mass.: Harvard University Press.

Scherer, F. 1980: *Industrial Market Structure and Economic Performance*, 2nd edn. Chicago: Rand-McNally.

Scherer, F. 1983: Regulatory dynamics and economic growth. In M. and S. Wachter (eds), *Towards a New US Industrial Policy?* Philadelphia: University of Pennsylvania Press.

Schiller, R. 1981: Do stock prices have too much variability to be justified by subsequent changes in dividends? *American Economic Review*, 71, 421–36.

Schmalensee, R. 1978: Entry deterrence in the ready-to-eat breakfast cereal industry. *Bell Journal of Economics*, 9, 305–27.

Sengupta, J., Leonard, J. and Vango, J. 1983: A limit pricing model for the US computer industry. *Applied Economics*, 15, 297–308.

Shaw, R. 1973: Investment and competition from boom to recession: a case study in the process of competition – the dry cleaning industry. *Journal of Industrial Economics*, 21, 308–24.

Shaw, R. 1974: Price leadership and the effect of new entry in the UK retail petrol supply market. *Journal of Industrial Economics*, 23, 65–79.

Shaw, R. 1980: New entry and the competitive process in the UK fertilizer industry. *Scottish Journal of Political Economy*, 27, 1–16.

Shaw, R. 1982: Product strategy and size of firm in the UK fertilizer market. *Managerial and Decision Economics*, 3, 233–43.

Shaw, R. and Shaw, S. 1977: Patent expiry and competition in polyester fibres. *Scottish Journal of Political Economy*, 24, 117–32.

Shaw, R. and Simpson, P. 1985a: The Monopolies Commission and the persistence of monopoly. *Journal of Industrial Economics*, 34, 355–72.

Shaw, R. and Simpson, P. 1985b: The Monopolies Commission and the process of competition. *Fiscal Studies*, 6, 82–96.

Shaw, R. and Sutton, C. 1976: *Industry and Competition*. London: Macmillan.

Shepherd, W. 1972: The elements of market structure. *Review of Economics and Statistics*, 54, 25–37.

Shepherd, W. 1975: *The Treatment of Market Power*. New York: Columbia University Press.

Stigler, G. 1965. The dominant firm and the inverted umbrella. *Journal of Law and Economics*. Reprinted in his *The Organization of Industry*, Homewood, Ill.: Irwin 108–12.

White, L. 1971: *The Automobile Industry since 1945*. Cambridge, Mass.: Harvard University Press.

Worcester, D. 1957: Why dominant firms decline. *Journal of Political Economy*, 65, 338–47.

Yamawaki, M. 1985: Dominant firm pricing and fringe expansion: the case of the US iron and steel industry, 1907–30. *Review of Economics and Statistics*, 67, 429–37.

Yip, G. 1982: *Barriers to Entry: a corporate strategy perspective*. Lexington, Mass.: Lexington Books.

Index

Index by Joyce Kerr